SOCIETY AND THE VICTORIANS
CONFESSIONS OF AN ECONOMIC HERETIC

CONFESSIONS OF AN ECONOMIC HERETIC

The Autobiography of

J. A. HOBSON

EDITED AND INTRODUCED BY
MICHAEL FREEDEN

THE HARVESTER PRESS

ARCHON BOOKS

This edition first published in 1976 by
THE HARVESTER PRESS LIMITED
Publisher: John Spiers
2 Stanford Terrace,
Hassocks, Nr Brighton
Sussex, England
and in the United States of America by
The Shoe String Press Inc.
Archon Books
Hamden, Connecticut 06514

'Confessions of an Economic Heretic' first published in 1938 by George Allen & Unwin Ltd, London

The Harvester Press Limited
ISBN 0 901759 91 0

The Shoestring Press, Inc.

Library of Congress Cataloging in Publication Data

Hobson, John Atkinson, 1858–1940.
Confessions of an economic heretic.

Reprint of the 1938 ed. published by G. Allen & Unwin, London.
1. Economics. 2. Social sciences. 3. Economic history—1918–1945. I. Title.
HB171.H647 1976 330.1 75–33279
ISBN 0–208–01579–5

Typesetting by Campbell Graphics Ltd., Newcastle upon Tyne
Printed in England by Biddles Ltd., Guildford

Introduction

Confessions of an Economic Heretic is not cast in the common mould of British autobiographical writing. It is neither a means to chronicle historical events nor a personal record of the author's life. Rather, it documents the intellectual history of one of Britain's leading modern social thinkers and, reflected through his perceptive eyes, the key socio-economic issues and ideas of an entire period. There can be no doubt to the modern scholar that J. A. Hobson (1858–1940) was not only—as the modest title of this book indicates—an iconoclast in the field of economic orthodoxy, but one of the architects of contemporary British social thought. The relative lack of familiarity of the public with Hobson's ideas and prolific written work has its roots in at least three factors. First, his inaccurate categorization as an economist or as a student of imperialism which, while in itself correct, cut him off from his main body of thought and obscured the importance of the general edifice he constructed. Secondly, the reluctance—until quite recently—of British scholarship to examine the role which ideas play in modern British political history—and here Hobson's contribution is immense. Thirdly, a point Hobson repeatedly dwelt upon in his *Confessions,* not without a hint of bitterness: The refusal of the British academic world to sanction his teachings and offer him a rostrum from which to diffuse them.

Though he himself did not make the claim, Hobson came very close to constructing a general system of thought through which human social behaviour could be analysed and explained. Besides being an active journalist, lecturer and social reformer, Hobson made important and original contributions to economics, political thought, international relations and sociology, dealing with all within a general, coherent and interrelated framework. He was above all an economic heretic in this wide sense. Contrary to 19th century practice he could not conceive of economics as a specialized discipline aspiring to the rank of an autonomous science. Instead, Hobson strove towards the crystallization of *a* social science, a unitary study of the processes of social evolution. He thus aligned himself with the tendency in British sociology at the turn of the century to formulate a general approach to the development of man in society. Spencer and, later, Hobhouse were Hobson's prime influences in this sphere. But Hobson's notion of society went further than either of theirs. It was based on two central concepts, humanism and organicism.

The first of these terms reflects the great impact Ruskin's writings had on shaping Hobson's thought (see Hobson's *John Ruskin Social Reformer* (1898)). Ruskin forcefully impressed upon Hobson that political economy (by then, as Hobson realized, hardly 'political') presented a false and partial picture of the nature and ends of economic activity. "Wealth is life" was the Ruskinian motto Hobson echoed and it involved a radical departure from contemporary economic maxims and methodology. The latter upheld the quantitative utilitarian viewpoint which put a premium upon the maximization of measurable wealth, thus singling out Economic Man as the archetype of a beneficial member of society. Hobson denied economic science—any science—the seal of authority which it claimed. Science, invariably associated by him with quantification, could not be used to measure the unmeasurable. Science had therefore to be subservient to art, to a qualitative conception of social life. Here was one of Hobson's fundamental messages to the modern world: the study of man cannot be value-free. Not only did the investigator approach his subject with certain aims in mind, but the subject-matter—man—could not be reduced to a measurable model without sacrificing its complexity. Above all, man was a thinker and a creator–his uniqueness lay in his ideas, his principles, his rational search for order and purpose. Hobson knew that in the vocation of social reformer clarification of the broad principles underlying human life had to precede action. The guiding criterion of human welfare entailed reference to an evolving and dynamic "trinity of forces"–economics, politics and ethics. Economics could not remain isolated from the attempts of organized humanity, via its political institutions, to improve the lot of the numerous citizens who were at a disadvantage under the competitive conditions of a free market or who, alternatively, were deprived of their freedom by powerful monopolies. But both economics and politics had to be guided by ethics in the sense of human valuations. This, then, was Hobson's humanism, as developed in a long list of books, notably *The Social Problem* (1901), *Work and Wealth* (1914), *Free Thought in the Social Sciences* (1926) and *Wealth and Life* (1929).

Hobson's second key notion, organicism, gave his concept of social utility its special meaning as standard of social action and infused the social ideas of the period with new blood. Hobson used 'organism' in three senses. Firstly, it served to remind his contemporaries that man was a biological organism. This truism must be set against the backdrop of Victorian morality, with its stress on the 'better self' and the 'higher realms' man's spirit was ordained to achieve. Not that this stress was discounted by Hobson. But in contrast to the high-handed attitude of institutions such as the Charity Organization Society he insisted that any conception of human welfare had to be grounded on man's physical needs. Such needs being standard, they could and had to be catered for by uniform and routine methods. The individual, as Hobson explained in *The Social Problem*, would consequently be released from material worries in order to realize his higher creative capacities. Only this combination could assure the optimization of welfare.

'Organic', however, meant something more. It was the clearest expression of Hobson's search for a 'total' viewpoint from which to perceive human activity. All activity—economic included—had to be regarded from the perspective of its total effect upon human life—the 'vital' standard. Hence cost was expenditure of life and utility its enrichment. This universalistic tendency explains why Hobson abhorred specialism—as a distorted separatism—and why he rejected all attempts to apply partial measures of social reform or to restrict them to limited social groups. Any class solution to the 'condition of the people' question was consequently ruled out.

This connects with the third usage of organicism: The description of society itself as an entity with a group-life and a collective consciousness. The organic analogy implies not only a state of mutual dependence among the parts of the whole but the assertion that the whole is not identical with the sum of the parts. By presenting the organic model as the essence of social life, Hobson supplied a conception of society diametrically opposed to the one prevailing in Britain before the end of the 19th century. The latter had posited an atomistic, self-interested aggregate of individuals whose limited interaction was determined and regulated chiefly by means of economic 'natural' laws. Hobson was instrumental in establishing the notion of community at the base of British socio-political thought. No less than Hobhouse, and perhaps more so, he was in the forefront of those who laid the ideological foundations of the welfare state and its redefinition of the relationship between individual and society.

Here theory combined with practice. For the best part of his life, until the first world war, Hobson belonged to the nucleus of a large and diversified group of progressive, reform-minded intellectuals—politicians, journalists, churchmen, social workers—who espoused what came to be known as the new liberalism. The Rainbow Circle, which published the *Progressive Review*, and the weekly *Nation* were foci of the intellectual activities of this group. The Ethical Movement, and, indeed, Oxford idealism operated on its periphery. The dramatic social legislation enacted by the Liberal party between 1908–14 owed much to progressive liberal thought. The party's later demise could not stem the momentum of the new liberalism, which to a large extent was preserved within a different framework, that of the Labour party. After the first world war many of the leading liberal intellectuals came to consider that organization as more capable of providing a platform for their ideas. Hence, what began as heresy—and not merely economic—in the 1890s grew to form part of the general consensus by the 1930s.

Adopting the notion of community entailed a reformulation of liberal principles. Hobson succeeded here in establishing a singularly apposite synthesis between the classic individualistic tenets of the old liberalism and the collectivist orientations of the new. The necessity for such a synthesis was pressing: The old *laissez-faire* ideology could not satisfy the social and intellectual needs of a highly industrialized nation with ever-growing circles of politically active citizens by whom conditions of living were considered intolerable and unjust. Hobson's work is important for attempting to meet this major challenge to the fabric and quality of British society. The organic conception of society was not used by him, as by so many of his predecessors, to assert the absolute priority of the group over the individual. It preserved a continuity with earlier liberalism by extolling the virtues of individuality rather than atomistic individualism. However, social, not individual, welfare was now seen to be the end of social organization. The balance between individual liberty and social utility was attained by encouraging individual development *because* such development benefited collective life. Without healthy parts there could be no healthy whole. Hobson presented these ideas convincingly in a collection of articles entitled *The Crisis of*

Liberalism (1909).[1]

All this necessitated the promotion of concerted social action, working through the organs of a state that expressed the collective will, not the interest of any class. The new confidence in state action now displayed by liberalism was a direct consequence of the redefinition of the social nature of man and of the equation of ethical life with the attainment of social health. Hobson's organicism implied a mutual responsibility among individuals and groups that was not philanthropy or charity but was dictated by the overall conception of social relationships. When translating this into social policy directives Hobson advocated a radical extension and intensification of the bonds between society and its members. The notion of community led to the idea of society as producer and creator of values. Taxation was primarily to be regarded as affirming this fact. Breaking with contract theory, Hobson interpreted the granting of individual 'rights' as a social act, intended to ensure the quality of social life by fulfilling the full range of human needs. The right to live was operationally reformulated as the right to subsistence. This was the precondition to participatory citizenship—the dynamic process of contributing to and benefiting from the fruits of society. The idea of a minimum standard of living which Hobson strongly advocated was a natural deduction from his own teachings. It was the conceptual meeting-point between the new social ethics and the liberal insistence on the importance for human development of competition, incentives and insulation from injurious social intervention. Socialism and individualism were united. Competition was rendered harmless by being restricted to operate above the minimum, i.e. the standard and the uniform. The Millian end of liberalism as individual perfection was set to a new use as the vehicle of the social good.

[1] Recently re-issued, edited by P. F. Clarke, in the 'Society & The Victorians' series (Brighton, The Harvester Press, 1974).

The rudimentary foundations of this conception had been laid before the first world war—old-age pensions, graduated taxation within the framework of a redistributionary budget, national health and unemployment insurance. The war itself had somewhat shaken Hobson's belief in human rationality as realizing itself along the path of social evolution, but one of its by-products was the great impetus given to state intervention and control. This was a congenial setting for the triumph of the ideas Hobson stood for before 1914. By the 1930s they had taken root: the era of public planning had come to stay, the vision of economic equality seemed somewhat more attainable, and new political and economic theories now found a ready ear.

The specific meaning of Hobson's economic heresy was indissolubly linked to his general analysis. The root social evil was, in his opinion, mal-distribution—the essence of the 'condition of the people' question and the antithesis of the true equality of economic opportunity on which the organic conception was based. Any valid economic science had therefore to grapple with this problem and this is what Hobson proceeded to do in a large number of works, the most prominent of which are *The Physiology of Industry* (with A. F. Mummery (1889)), *The Problem of the Unemployed* (1896) and *The Industrial System* (1909). Here, too, Hobson challenged the Victorian moral-economic injunction of thrift. The concentration of 19th-century economics on production and savings Hobson regarded as insufficient. He was more concerned with the phenomena of over-saving, over-production and under-consumption. Here was the cause of the recurrent crises of the capitalist system, brought about by a disruption of the correct saving-spending ratio necessary to maintain equilibrium in the processes of production and consumption. Under-consumption was the result of an unequal distribution of the power to consume. The rich had more than they needed and could not consume beyond saturation point. Their surplus income from whatever source belonged to society, the principal creator of values, and had to be put to social use. The low income of the poor meant a lack of demand for goods, resulting in a glut of commodities and consequently in a standstill of capital and labour. Only state intervention in the form of a redistribution of income could remedy the inequality and inequity of the market situation (organized labour was too self-interested to pursue universal social ends). Even from a narrow economic perspective the issue of poverty did not concern only those involved, but the nation at large. Raising the material and intellectual level of the poor and thus increasing their propensity and capacity to consume would result in fuller employment and keep the wheels of industry turning. The cohesion of Hobson's thought is further evident if one notes that this remedy would also remove the pressure for foreign markets which lay at the root of imperialism and international competition. Hobson's *Imperialism* (1902), which in itself established his reputation, was but a link in a wider chain.

Though Hobson was criticized for failing to distinguish properly between saving and investment and for disregarding monetary explanations of the crises of capitalism, he nevertheless provided a scientific basis for the social reformers' crusade against the economic misery of the masses. His ethical condemnation, as social reformer, of the quality of social life was thus bolstered by his rejection, as economist, of some of the principal tenets on which that science was based. He denied that production and distribution were self-adjusting mechanisms and disputed the economic rationality of a competitive market. This ran contrary to the prevailing assumption (known as Say's law) that production created its own demand.

Of all the major British economists, only Keynes recognized the merits of Hobson's theories. Hobson preceded the Keynesian revolution not only in his grasp of the nature of unemployment but in his insistence that state regulation was an indispensable factor of the economic system. Though these theories were only implemented by the Labour government after 1945, Hobson became in the eve of his life one of the leading influences on the Labour party, even if he himself stopped short of its comprehensive socialist outlook. His advocacy of nationalization of key monopolies and of routine industries had ceased to be regarded as the demands of an extremist fringe. Considerable progress had been made towards realizing his concept of economic democracy—the collective planning of economic life with a view to ethical ends.

The fact that Hobson was a firm believer in the harnessing of state organs to pursue the social good could, of course, pose some problems for a society steeped in a voluntaristic and decentralized tradition and more averse than not to planning. Hobson never failed to stress that political democracy could only be sustained by collective control over basic economic processes. But his ideas on political organization often had non-democratic undertones. There was more than a hint of a meritocracy in Hobson's respect for the 'disinterested expert'. His preoccupation with a social mind deflected him from the traditional liberal path with its emphasis on individual choice and self-determination. Rationalism had to supersede commonsense. The long view of the state—as agent of the social organism—was beyond the grasp of the partial view of any unit. Authoritative expertise was yet another manifestation of the 'responsible society' Hobson was aiming at. But at the same time he knew that it also had to be a 'responsive society', for economic democracy demanded the extension of popular control over actions undertaken for the citizens and on their behalf, as well as the channelling of those displays of public-spiritedness exhibited by politically conscious individuals.

Hobson was eighty years old when the *Confessions* were published. His lucid style and balanced exposition, which make the book invaluable as an introduction to his thought, showed no signs of flagging. Though he received a certain amount of recognition in his old age—in the words of G. P. Gooch, as 'representative of the Elder Statesmen of the

Republic of Thought'—the time has come to accord him a permanent place of honour among the social, political and economic thinkers who were the driving intellectual force behind modern liberal social-democracy.

Michael Freeden

CONFESSIONS OF AN ECONOMIC HERETIC

FOREWORD

AUTOBIOGRAPHY is often considered to be the least defensible form of biography, because it is impossible to see ourselves as others see us, and a skilled onlooker is more likely to see us right. Against this, however, may be set two considerations. Certain relevant facts, with special bearing on a man's thought and feelings, can only come into his personal knowledge. And, again, in the almost inevitable attempt to make the best of himself, an autobiographer is pretty certain to "give himself away" by processes of selection, concealment, and over-emphasis which are discerned by the unbiased reader and shed important light upon the mind and character of the "life" in question.

Both of these considerations are especially applicable to the restricted type of autobiography recorded here. For, while primarily directed to explaining the development of my economic thinking during half a century, it is largely engaged in showing how that thinking has been affected by current events and personal experiences that lie outside the accepted field of economics, some of them quite momentous in their impact on my mental career, others belonging to fields of experience which accepted political economy does not recognize as having any bearing on its special study. I have taken the title of heretic not in the spirit of bravado, but because it strictly applies to the several processes of thought which have come to debar me from accepting the assumptions regarding the nature of such terms as "value," "cost," "utility" as are still fixed in the orthodox economics of our time. In my endeavour to give a human interpretation to such terms and to the processes in which they figure, and to establish a basis of harmony between the arts of industry thus humanized, and other arts of personal and social conduct, political, ethical, artistic, recreative, which utilize the fruits of industry, I claim to have made some advance towards a better understanding of the part played by economic thinking and economic practices in a world of changing environment and values. It belongs, however, to the account I give of the thinking process, to admit that I may be biased in favour of the rightness and the worth of such a claim.

CONTENTS

CHAPTER I

CLASS INFLUENCES IN EARLY YOUTH

SOME years ago I was foolish enough to write a long book entitled *Free Thought in the Social Sciences*,* setting forth the difficulties that confronted thinkers and teachers in history, politics, economics, ethics, and other studies of human institutions and conduct, because of the refractory nature of the material they handled, the defects of terminology, and in particular the biases of interest and valuation due to their own personal experiences and associations. I ought to have known that any such argument, questioning the objectivity and disinterestedness of these studies, and so damaging their scientific reputation, would be ignored, not refuted. For if my reasoning were correct, it would disturb that intellectual confidence regarding fundamentals which seems essential to maintain the laborious study of the detailed facts. If it be true that the intellectual exponents of the sciences of politics and economics in particular are secretly, perhaps subconsciously, aware of the uncertainty of their main assumptions and of the pressure of their personal or class sentiments and valuations, they will struggle to repress these doubts and questionings and to keep a stiff intellectual upper lip. For the committal to, and

* London: George Allen & Unwin, Ltd.

the defence of, dubious assumptions arouse a sense of intellectual property which the owners cannot bear to see depreciated, and for the maintenance of which they will fight with every weapon at their disposal. But the best weapon is a refusal to discuss, or to refute, because the issue is already settled and beyond dispute. This dogmatic atmosphere is not, of course, confined to the social sciences. It has always impeded progress in the physical sciences, especially in those organic sciences which, like biology, claim to throw light upon the nature and behaviour of man. But in the more exact sciences, where false or outworn laws or hypotheses can definitely be refuted and replaced by others, there is little of that emotional strain that comes when an economic law or a political principle is challenged. Only so far as beliefs concerning the physical world have been incorporated in religious creeds has an aura of sanctity attached to them which has made their denial an act of wickedness. In modern times this attitude has been so modified in most countries that the revolutionary physics of an Einstein are received with little intellectual or emotional difficulty (outside Hitler's Germany), and Darwinism, though fiercely denounced in its early days, has, except in Fundamentalist circles, won place in an orthodoxy remodelled for its acceptance.

The case is, however, very different for new controversial issues in the fields of politics and economics.

As religious faith and sectarian controversy are weakened, this world displacing the next in most men's minds, an intensification of passion has entered into the secular movements for reform and the "isms" which they incorporate and endeavour to express. A number of new passionate creeds and movements, appealing to the reason, justice, and welfare of mankind, to the interests of individuals, classes, nations, races, and humanity, are struggling to gain power over human conduct in the arts of economic and political organization. These new appeals and movements have so reacted upon orthodox ideas, interests, and parties, as to infuse a new vigour of resistance into the latter, in which a discreet policy of minor concessions and adaptations to new social circumstances is used to strengthen the buttresses of the nineteenth-century conservatism and liberalism. For the assailant "isms," Fascism, Socialism, Communism, in their several sorts and qualities, have sprung up with unexpected rapidity in a world where a generation ago peace, progress, security, and general contentment seemed to be the accepted ways of life, and where minor troubles seemed capable of cheap and easy settlement. In politics, popular self-government (under the actual control of ruling groups or families), in economics the growing application of equality of opportunity (within reasonable limits) were, up to the last decade of the nineteenth century, held to be sufficient guarantees for a pacific, prosperous future in all countries which had ranged themselves along self-governing lines.

Now it is no part of my intention here to engage upon the large task of a general explanation of the recent rapid changes in policy and thinking. For holding, as I do, that man is not a very reasonable animal, but is to a larger extent than he likes to admit the servant of his personal short-range interests and passions, it would be of little service to try to argue out the inflammatory issues in politics and economics. This criticism, moreover, applies not only to the mass of mankind, but with some special significance to those who think for them and mould their thinking into principles and policies. It is, indeed, the play of tradition, class feeling, and interests upon the thinkers who regard themselves as disinterested rationalists that here concerns me.

But for my purpose a further narrowing process is required. Since I shall be engaged in work of social criticism, I must myself be exposed to those deflecting influences that operate on others, and though it is not possible to pretend to an impartiality and objectivity which I deny to others, it is possible for me to trace and set forth in my own intellectual career some of the causal and casual occurrences which have determined my own thinking during a period of more than half a century.

While the more formal processes of acquiring knowledge belong to the education of school or college, the elementary facts and feelings related to our family and other social surroundings are drawn almost insensibly into our childish minds from our immediate environment, with such parental suggestions as may be brought into play. The total influence of these early happenings and feelings is now recognized as extremely important in determining the later conscious thinking upon all personal and social problems. Where some great social event, such as a war, pestilence, or famine, breaks in upon the experience of childhood, it leaves a crop of passions, fears, and tumultuous feelings which gravely affect all processes of thinking in matters affecting personal and social conduct. This platitude I repeat because it has a definite bearing on my early years which were cast in the calmest and most self-confident years of the mid-Victorian era, when peace, prosperity, and progress appeared to be the permanent possession of most civilized nations. Born and bred in the middle stratum of the middle class of a middle-sized industrial town of the Midlands, I was favourably situated for a complacent acceptance of the existing social order. There was not stagnation anywhere, but a gradual orderly improvement in the standard of living, the working conditions, and the behaviour of most classes. The social stratification was taken for granted, there was no serious attempt of the working classes to push their economic or social claims upon the upper classes. Energetic or able individuals could use their opportunities to rise, and a few of the wealthiest families had "risen from the ranks." But in general the social and the economic classification was identical. As a "county" town Derby held among its residents a few remnants of aristocratic families, which mixed somewhat shyly with a small upper middle class composed of the pick of the professions, clergy, doctors, and lawyers, and leading officials of the town. The general run of professional men and the more prosperous manufacturers or wholesale merchants formed a social class, less fixed in personnel, but quite distinct from the retail traders whose name over their shops kept them on a definitely lower social level, though their incomes and education were hardly distinguishable from the professional strata. Clerks in banks and offices had a lower measure of precarious respectability, but were distinguishable from all grades of manual workers. The bulk of these latter were employees of the Midland Railway or of the new manufactures that were springing up to replace the earlier and now decaying textile factories. At the bottom of the social-industrial ladder was a considerable batch of poor, irregular workers, largely of Irish origin, many of whom occupied a street bearing the sinister title "Back Lane." The poverty of these families was attributed by common consent to their shiftless, thriftless, reckless way of living, and formed a difficult problem not of social management but of charity. I well recollect the ragged, shoeless condition of the children of these "poor." They stirred in me not so much a sense of pity or of distress as of an incipient feeling that "all was not right" in this best of all possible worlds. But I would not assign this feeling as a definite seed of economic thought. For it was far later that I came to concern myself with "problems of poverty."

Perhaps a more suggestive feeling of this boyhood was addressed to the other end of the social economic scale as it was exhibited in my native town. I refer to the push and sagacity by which half a dozen men, who had attained considerable wealth in manufacture and commerce, used their generosity to local charities and their political pressure to obtain knighthoods, so rising out of the ruck of their social competitors into a level beyond mere "respectability."

Politics in this placid epoch had little social or economic significance. Factory legislation and other interference with competitive capitalism did not figure with any prominence, and, though there was a good deal of loose philanthropic talk about "the amelioration of the condition of the working classes," there was no sincere attempt at amelioration by governmental action. The dominant classes in Derby were pretty equally divided between Conservatism and Liberalism, the latter generally carrying the elections by their larger hold upon the working-class electors. When I first began 'to take notice' of such matters as elections, Gladstone and Disraeli were the great protagonists, while conflicts where the extension of the franchise, popular education, Irish land tenure, non-conformist rating, with something called the Eastern question, were the main staple of party politics. The Franco-German War of 1870 was happily kept out of English politics, and though the disestablishment of the English Church and even a spasm of Republicanism under the leadership of Dilke and Bradlaugh began to agitate a handful of "radicals" in most English towns, they did not disturb the main body of respectable Liberals. In my earliest recollection, the two Liberal members for the town were Bass and Beale, both men of means and high social standing. The first breach in high respectability was an intrusion of the semi-radical Samuel Plimsoll, felt by my father and other sober Liberals to be a somewhat dangerous innovation. But the real point of significance is that, though born and bred in an atmosphere of active Liberalism (our livelihood drawn from the conduct of a "liberal" newspaper), I had no idea, as a boy, that politics had anything to do with industry or standards of living. Nor was this merely a failure to understand a really intricate relation. At that time the two-party system was engaged half-consciously in keeping out of politics all deep and drastic issues of "the condition of the people." Throughout his long career of public service Gladstone kept Liberalism upon issues of franchise, education, public economy, and foreign policy, hardly touching any of the graver economic issues, except when they impinged upon his Irish policy. This *laisser-faire* attitude of the Liberalism of the sixties and seventies was the accepted basis of my earliest political education. The gulf between politics and workaday life was fixed and complete.

But two other lines of personal experience bearing upon class distinctions had some influence in the early moulding of my social thinking. Derby was a religious community in which the Established Church and leading Nonconformist sects were strongly supported. Church and chapel going was universal and, for the young, compulsory: family prayers were pretty general, and piety played a considerable part in ordinary life. But though in creed there was little divergence, the social cleavage between Church people and Dissenters was clear and strong. A higher grade of respectability attached to the former, and there was a tendency for the younger generation of well-to-do Dissenters to join the Church when they reached "years of discretion." Church and Dissent upon the whole meant rich and poor, though most dissenting chapels were necessarily financed by fairly well-to-do members. I noticed also a certain favourable social discrimination in favour of Quakers and Unitarians, based, I suppose, upon the fact that in those small sects a larger proportion of the followers were recognized as men and women of good social and financial standing.

Ritualism was slow to enter into our church services even in the late sixties. Though Derby had its Catholic

Church, it was an alien body, mainly Irish and with virtually no intercourse, moral or social, with other churches. I was brought up in a moderate puritanism which eschewed all taint of Romanism. One of my earliest clear religious memories is that of being "walked out" of church with the rest of my family because the Vicar for the first time appeared in a white surplice instead of a black gown. My father, who was a churchwarden, on reaching home wrote a strong letter of expostulation, and after a brief interval in a dull little church under a minister of dubious character, we settled down in the church which is now Derby Cathedral, under the ministry of a famous evangelical preacher, the Rev. Sholto Douglas Campbell Douglas, who for some years oversatisfied our religious ardour by sermons of an hour and a quarter. In these years a strain of active piety took me away from this world's thoughts, engaging me in serious endeavours to realize the meaning of the creeds and prayers placed before my childish mind. The failure to satisfy my elementary sense of reason and of justice in the doctrines of the atonement and of everlasting punishment for unrepentant sinners were, I think, the earliest evidence of a humanism which in early manhood led me to the abandonment of orthodox Christianity. At the time it was a painful process of an intellectual failure to reconcile tenets I was brought up to reverence with the dictates of my personal conscience. By the time I reached Oxford I found myself a religious heretic and in my second year obtained a remission of the duty to attend chapel. It is perhaps worthy of mention that the earliest of my published writings consisted of two articles in the *Westminster Review*, dealing with religious topics, one entitled "Dr. Temple on Religion and Science" (discussing his heretical paper in *Essays and Reviews*), the other "Mr. Gladstone and Genesis."

My education in the local Grammar School under a head master who hastened to shed the low title "Grammar," and to convert the school into a public school, with a reputable body of boarders to qualify the "local" dependence, helped me to some further understanding of social-economic distinctions. For the head master was a persistent "snob" of the crudest order. A classical scholar with no taste for literature, he devoted his teaching energy into imposing the prestige of the dead languages upon as many boys as possible, irrespective of their tastes or aptitudes. Mathematics was taught with "scholarship" success to a little group of able boys, including my elder brother, afterwards a Professor of Mathematics at Cambridge. The natural sciences comprised a little chemistry, less physics, and virtually no biology. History was almost entirely English, stopped dead before modern politics began to emerge, and consisted only of the dramatic activities of kings and the ruling classes. A minimum of ancient history accompanied the classics. There was nowhere any attempt to shed light upon current institutions and events. The notion of citizenship as a subject for education never occurred to any teacher and would have been dismissed as unmeaning. Modern languages consisted of a little French, but no German. Sport was encouraged as a means of bringing us into the company of more reputable public schools on a basis of equality. "Speech days," presided over by some carefully netted celebrity, conduced to the same end. The head master's most signal achievement was the presence at the speech day in 1873 of the Prince of Wales, who happened to be a guest of "the Duke" at Chatsworth. My memory of that event is registered in a prize for "Divinity" bestowed by the royal hand. It was long before the full humour of this proceeding came home to me. The great literature of my native land was confined to a linguistic study of a play or two of Shakespeare, forced upon us by the requirements of the Cambridge Junior or Senior Certificate examination, and a bit of Milton, or of Tennyson, set for a "holiday task." My fairly large private reading of Shakespeare, Milton, and my favourite Pope, with Bacon's *Essays* and Boswell's *Johnson*, was a blend of genuine appreciation and personal "swank," how much of each it is difficult to judge, as I look back upon my early "education."

Not until my later schooldays in the mid-seventies did my mind touch any economic or other social study. Somehow occasional essay-writing was introduced into the sixth form, as serviceable for winning a University scholarship, and an Oxford Don, chosen for the purpose, set me upon Mill's *Liberty* and *Utilitarianism*, which caught my sympathy as a budding rationalist. How Spencer's *Study of Sociology* came into my hands I cannot recollect, though it exercised a profound influence in suggesting that social institutions could rightly come within the ambit of interesting study. Possibly the knowledge that Spencer was himself born and reared in Derby stimulated my curiosity. For, as a boy in my early teens, I used to meet Spencer walking into town with a man named Lott, a bank manager and a close friend of his. But while I had some slight acquaintance with Lott, I never exchanged a word with Spencer, though some quarter of a century later we interchanged letters upon the subject of the Boer War.

My first definite approach to Economics was by way of the Cambridge University Extension Movement of the seventies. One of the earliest of these Courses was in Derby, and in 1875 I attended lectures on political economy, wrote weekly papers, and took the examination. Our text-books were Mill and Mrs. Fawcett, with, I think, a few chapters of Adam Smith. J. S. Mill was the "authority," for his statement in 1848 that, "Happily there is nothing in the laws of Value, which remains for the present or any future writer to clear up," still held the academic field, though W. S. Jevons's *Theory of Political Economy* had appeared some years ago (in 1871). From this early study I learned that, in the sphere of activity which absorbed most of the thought, interest, and energy of all our population, except a small leisure class, principles and laws governed the production and distribution of wealth which intelligent men and women accepted as belonging to the order of Nature. They established the justice, necessity, and finality of the existing economic system.* But, while accepting these

* This was not, of course, the personal attitude of J. S. Mill. Even in his *Political Economy* of 1848 he indulged in speculations of a socialistic future. "The form of association—which, if mankind continues to improve, must be expected in the end to predominate, is not that which can exist between a capitalist as chief, and work-people without a voice in the management, but the association of the labourers themselves on terms of equality, collectively owning the capital with which they carry on their operations, and working under managers elected and removable by themselves" (Bk. VI, chapter viii, § 6).

In his *Autobiography* (1871) he explains more explicitly his breakaway from Benthamism with its economic doctrines, and expressly adopts the title Socialist. "The social problem of the future we considered to be, how to unite the greatest individual liberty of action, with a common ownership in the raw material of the globe, and an equal participation of all in the benefits of combined labour" (p. 232).

But the academic Political Economy of the day continued to concern itself with the exposition of the laws of current industry, and disregarded these speculative aberrations, just as it had swept into the rubbish heap the early nineteenth-century English works on Socialism, dug out by H. S. Foxwell in his Introduction to Menger's *The Right to the Whole Produce of Labour*. Not until much later on did I realize how potent was the influence of victorious capitalism to impress the justice and utility of its procedure upon principles and laws in the spirit of a true believer, I discovered later on that a seed of doubt had been sown in my mind which was destined to bear perilous fruit. For Mill's dogma that "A demand for commodities is not a demand for labour," plausibly supported by the teaching that all wages were paid from a "fund" that represented a portion of past savings, seems even at that early time to have stuck in my gizzard.

It was, however, not until the middle eighties that my economic heterodoxy began to take shape. At Oxford in the late seventies I made no serious attempt at economic study, for Modern Greats did not then exist, and Classical Greats had no room for it. Some part I took in College debates upon Fair Trade which was the first phase in the later campaign of Protectionism, and though attending with regularity the Union debates, where economics occasionally butted into politics, I heard nothing to disturb my complacent acceptance of the beneficent and equitable operation

the dawning science of Economics and to exclude from consideration all attempts to challenge its intellectual domination. When the leading nineteenth-century economists are accused of inhumanity and lack of sympathy with working-class aspirations, it is possible in most cases from Ricardo onwards, to cite passages which refute this accusation. But the substance of the accusation remains untouched. For these humanist *obiter dicta* were never incorporated in the body of their economic teaching which was always directed towards establishing natural laws of price and value in production and distribution aiming more and more at quantitative exactitude.

of laws of supply and demand in their *laisser-faire* environment.

Four years at Oxford, chiefly spent on the literary, historical, and philosophical study of the Latin and Greek civilizations, contributed, however, not a little towards the rationalism and humanism which later on I strove to apply to economics. Some humanity may be got out of the study of *Literae Humaniores*. Though my failure as an examinee came as a painful shock to my intellectual self-assurance, it did not wholly disable me from receiving the contributions which Plato and Aristotle made to the permanent possessions of the human mind, what to think and feel, how to think and feel, about man's inner nature and his place in the universe, and the methods of testing and achieving knowledge. Though I never became a profound student of ancient thought and literature, I think that my mind received from these years of study a disposition and a valuation that were of immense service in liberating me from the easy acceptance of the current ideas and feelings of an age rightly designated as materialistic and narrowly utilitarian. Something more I feel that I received from the atmosphere of an Oxford in which Jowett, T. H. Green, and Mark Pattison were leading figures, though my only personal contact, not a close one, was with Pattison, the master of my college, in his declining years.

CHAPTER II

AN EARLY HERESY

In my early approaches towards economic study it had struck me as odd that the private ownership of land and the receipt of its rent seemed a matter of no importance to our political economists. Failing to recognize that rent played any part as a cost of production, they simply accepted it as belonging to the order of nature, beneficial no doubt to its recipients, but not injurious to anybody else. Not until Henry George stirred the issue up to boiling-point in his *Progress and Poverty* did the inequity of private ownership of the earth get much attention, and even then it suffered the damage that comes from exaggeration and panaceic simplicity. For the contention that the whole gains of the Industrial Revolution were absorbed by private landowners was far less plausible in England than in America. The career of this doctrine is, indeed, an interesting testimony to the *naïveté* of the British mind. It never was accepted as a working-class creed. Its followers here were mostly middle-class townsmen affected by personal knowledge of local cases of land-increments. Little knots of such men, to whom the single-tax or other device for confiscation of land-values is the all-sufficient gospel of social reform, linger on into the present day. One aspect of this tenacity must not, however, be ignored. By concentrating upon a single form of unearned wealth it enables its adherents to evade and arrest the wider claims of Socialism. "A single-taxer" is free to take every economic advantage he may enjoy as capitalist, employer, investor, in dealing with weaker bargainers. While the landowner's income is wholly unearned, his own business gains are the product of his skill, industry, foresight!

I was never a convinced single-taxer, for the early eighties ushered in more momentous issues in the exposure of poverty, by Charles Booth and his collaborators, and by the more sensational revelations of the other Booth's *In Darkest England*. The growing sense of poverty with its physical and moral evils as a social disease, and not as an individual fault or misfortune, may be traced to these investigators. But they did not stand alone. They belonged to a widespread breakdown of what is termed the mid-Victorian complacency, and evoked other protests of a wider and more active character. Modern English Socialism dated from this period as an organized conscious movement. The Fabian Society with its intellectuals, the Social Democratic Society of Hyndman and its breakaway group under William Morris, expressed a varied protest, rationalistic, ethical, political, aesthetic against the sort of civilization that was emerging under mechanized capitalism. There was also a small but active group of Christian Socialists, persisting in the belief that it might be possible to square the plain teaching of Christ with the practical teaching and conduct of British Christianity in its mundane aspect. But though I felt a certain sympathy with all those movements, attended their gatherings, and became acquainted with some of their leaders, I joined none of them. For, with the exception of the Fabians, they appeared to me either too inflammatory or too sentimental. Even the Fabians did not, in my judgment, assail capitalism in its weakest points, and though the *Fabian Essays** were a notable contribution to the economic education of the open-minded few, they had not the spirit of a popular appeal. The time for an effective general challenge of Capitalism was not yet ripe. Revelations of poverty, together with the extension of trade unionism to the unskilled workers (dramatized in the Dock Strike of 1889), were the direct stimuli of the "social reforms" of the nineties, and brought into being the Labour Party, which was soon to assume the name, if not the substance, of Socialism. But though my opinions and my feelings were beginning to move in the direction of Socialism, I was not a Socialist, Marxian, Fabian, or Christian.

Long before my mind was free to work upon the fundamental issues of economic science, I was caught in the network of a narrower economic heresy which played a distinctive part in all my later thinking. It came from what may be called an accidental contact.

* London: The Fabian Society and George Allen & Unwin, Ltd.

While teaching at a school in Exeter I came into personal relations with a business man named Mummery, known then and afterwards as a great mountaineer who had discovered another way up the Matterhorn and who in 1895 was killed in an attempt to climb the famous Himalayan mountain Nanga Parbat. My intercourse with him, I need hardly say, did not lie on this physical plane. But he was a mental climber as well, with a natural zest for a path of his own finding and a sublime disregard of intellectual authority. This man entangled me in a controversy about excessive saving, which he regarded as responsible for the under-employment of capital and labour in periods of bad trade. For a long time I sought to counter his arguments by the use of the orthodox economic weapons. But at length he convinced me and I went in with him to elaborate the over-saving argument in a book entitled *The Physiology of Industry*, which was published in 1889. This was the first open step in my heretical career, and I did not in the least realize its momentous consequences. For just at that time I had given up my scholastic post and was opening a new line of work as University Extension Lecturer in Economics and Literature. The first shock came in a refusal of the London Extension Board to allow me to offer courses of political economy. This was due, I learned, to the intervention of an economic Professor who had read my book and considered it as equivalent in rationality to an attempt to prove the flatness of the earth. How could there be any limit to the amount of useful saving when every item of saving went to increase the capital structure and the fund for paying wages? Sound economists could not fail to view with horror an argument which sought to check the source of all industrial progress. Another interesting personal experience helped to bring home to me the sense of my iniquity. Though prevented from lecturing on economics in London, I had been allowed by the greater liberality of the Oxford University Extension Movement to address audiences in the provinces, confining myself to practical issues relating to working-class life. Now it happened at this time that the Charity Organisation Society was planning a lecture campaign upon economic subjects and invited me to prepare a course. For I had already been associated with the London Ethical Society, several active members of which were also workers for the C.O.S. I had expressed my willingness to undertake this new lecture work, when suddenly, without explanation, the invitation was withdrawn. Even then I hardly realized that in appearing to question the virtue of unlimited thrift I had committed the unpardonable sin.

I may here interpose the statement that my heresy was far from being as original a sin as I had supposed. For, as Mr. J. M. Robertson has shown in his book *The Fallacy of Saving*, the heresy had a fairly long record in the annals of English economic thinking, including in its adherents such reputable names as Shaftesbury,

Berkeley, and Malthus. Nevertheless, it remained an offence against the new science built up in the nineteenth century for the explanation, the defence, and the glorification of the era of capitalism which had transformed the modes of manufacture, commerce, and communications and appeared to justify itself by an illimitable increase of wealth—for those who were in charge of the new processes. For these processes of capitalistic production were dependent upon a constantly increasing provision of new capital and, therefore, upon the willingness of an increasing number of persons to save and invest income which they might have spent in raising their standard of comfort and luxury.

So it came about that the heresy of over-saving committed a deadly offence. It contravened the one claim which political economy had to ethical respectability. For the "economic man," though consciously moved by intelligent self-interest in the pursuit of personal gain, was led "as by an invisible hand" to a line of conduct conducive to the welfare of the community. He could, therefore, figure as a benevolent or kindly being. For it was his function to keep down the costs of production, including wages, to the lowest level, in order that the product of industry should be as large as possible.

It was difficult for students of this economic theory to gloss over its essential selfishness by adducing passages from the writings of economists which show gleams of liberality and humanity. The cold truth remained that the *laisser-faire* theory of competitive capitalism which exists even to-day in the seats of economic authority rested upon a foundation of intelligent selfishness. Nor was this selfishness redeemed by other personal qualities of economic efficiency, such as honesty within the limits of the law, industry, initiative, constructive and administrative ability. All these qualities are admirable in themselves and helpful towards personal success. But they do not carry the badge of ethical goodness. Now the personal self-sacrifice of thrift and saving, the postponement of present satisfaction to the needs of the future and the furtherance of larger human requirements—here was a definitely moral quality. Though the Charity Organisation Society approached the subject from a somewhat different angle, stressing less the public utility of thrift and more the personal element in character, it is easy to see how both the economist and the charity organizer felt and thought that any teaching which seemed to reflect on the utility or the virtue of personal thrift must be discouraged.

I found, and still find, it idle to protest that my argument against over-saving was not directed against individual thrift, that it left it open to any thrifty individual to spend as little as he chose of his income and to save as much. Any individual may starve himself and his family and put aside three-quarters of his income against future contingencies which may never arise, if he is fool enough to do so. Nay, a whole group, even a nation, may commit this folly if they choose. Soviet Russia went a considerable way along this foolish path when they strove to put their country-workers on or below starvation rations in order to expedite the creation of industrial capital, an impolicy which they have now had sense enough to correct. But the fallacy of unlimited saving in this country was left undetected for the greater part of a century, for this reason. If Britain had been an isolated economic community (as now too late we are seeking to become) we should have been brought up against the limit of effective saving long ago. But so long as we were the only advanced industrial country with a large exportable surplus, there was no limit to our profitable saving. Any nation, like any individual, may save all it chooses, provided other nations are not able or willing to follow the same policy. It was only when Germany, America, France, and Japan began to encroach upon our practical monopoly of the world market for the export of staple manufactures and for the capital development of backward countries, that the fallacy of unlimited saving became apparent. It is at root a very simple fallacy, viz. the contention that what anyone can do, all can do. The doctrine of human equality used to be driven home in American schools by reminding a class that any boy might become President of the United States. But no credence would have attached to the statement that all the boys might win the Presidential post.

This country had grown so accustomed to the position of chief exporter and developer of backward lands that it is still difficult both for our capitalists and their economists to realize the momentous change that has taken place when a dozen other countries can compete with us on equal, sometimes superior, terms. The lesson, however, is everywhere being driven home for those who have thrown off the thraldom of the old political economy, and are able to put together the two salient economic facts of our time, the unprecedented unemployment and the movement of every country towards economic isolationism and protection of home markets.

This is not, however, clearly discernible in my first solid piece of economic writing in the early nineties, my *Evolution of Modern Capitalism*,* an objective presentation of the industrial changes comprised under the Industrial Revolution in its British shape. Though I had read the English translation of Marx's first volume of *Das Kapital* some years before, I made no attempt to assess the value of his revolutionary attack. I was deterred, in part, by what still seems to me his false endeavour to express all costs of production in terms of units of labour-time, a common measure which could never operate in actual industry; in part, by a Hegelian dialectic which used an empty intellectual

* London: George Allen & Unwin, Ltd.

paradox to impart an air of mysticism into quite intelligible historic processes. My "Capitalism" ignored all theory that did not present itself in the actual processes which I studied. The chief significance lay in its claim to be a scientific study, as contained in the *Contemporary Science Series*. My part in its production was almost a matter of chance. It was put upon me by my friend, William Clarke, one of the Fabian Essayists, who, after undertaking to write it, found that the labours of his journalistic career precluded fulfilment of his undertaking. Having more time at my disposal, and finding that the study was definitely useful for my lecture work, I took it in hand. The main part of the book was given to an account of the rôle played by modern machinery and power in enlarging the productivity of industry, increasing the importance of the employer, the organizer, and the owner of capital, in the economy of labour and the control of markets. The nature of most work, the conditions under which it was done, and the payment for it, were determined by the employer in all mechanized industries, and a new proletariat came into existence, divorced alike from all personal control of other factors of production than labour, and devoted to the performance of some single narrow action contributing to a complex co-operative process of production which had no human concern for the great mass of wage-earners. Although the story of these economic changes necessarily involved some account of the quantitative relations between the volume of production and of consumption in the social industries and in the economic system as a whole (thus compelling a restatement of my "heresy" of over-saving), I did not yet fully explore the saving and the spending processes so as to make over-saving a necessary implication of capitalism.

Though there was nothing novel in my survey of capitalism, it became an educational textbook in some colleges here and in America, and helped in some measure to cover up the discredit of my earlier work and almost to win for me a place of academic respectability. Yet, as I look back upon it, I find that it contains in germ nearly all the departures from economic orthodoxy which my subsequent writings disclosed.

CHAPTER III

HUMANISM AND RATIONALISM

THE two main lines of this departure lie in the development of a "humanist" interpretation of the processes of production and consumption, and in the revolt against the accepted theory of *laisser-faire* as a security for the welfare of the community regarded as a productive and consumptive whole.

The need for the humanization of economic science and art was intensified by the study which I gave to Ruskin in the mid-nineties. Here again the initiative was not mine but came from Sir Charles Mallet, who asked me to write the book which I published in 1898 under the title *John Ruskin; Social Reformer*. I had read and admired *Unto this Last** some years before, but had regarded it rather as a passionate rebellion than as a critical and constructive work. The violence of its assault upon modern processes and the demand for "captains of industry" to dominate economic life repelled me. But when I took it up again and read it in conjunction with *Munera Pulveris*,* which sets forth in logical order Ruskin's claim to be a scientific thinker, I recognized that his insistence upon interpreting the terms "wealth" and "value" in their proper meanings "welfare" and "vitality" was not

* London: George Allen & Unwin, Ltd.

the mere freak of a literary verbalist but a genuinely scientific demand. "There is no wealth but life. Life including all its powers of love, of joy, and of admiration. That country is the richest which nourishes the greatest number of noble and happy human beings; that man is richest who, having perfected the functions of his own life to the utmost, has also the widest influence, both personal and by means of his possessions, over the lives of others."* Here, as elsewhere, the rich and impassioned eloquence of Ruskin was, and still is, an obstacle to his acceptance as a scientific teacher in a country where every form of eloquence is still apt to be regarded with suspicion as an attempt to cloud our reason. But Ruskin's main charge against the current political economy was that it had deliberately and systematically degraded the true and formerly accepted meaning of such terms as "wealth," "value," and "profit" by putting them to the narrow service of business mentality.

Though Ruskin often protested that his indictment was "scientific," it can hardly be questioned that it derived its force and validity from his appreciation of life as the finest of the fine arts. This required him to introduce the ethical standard of an "ought" into the valuation of every economic process or result. I expressed this important need in the following passage of my book. "The true 'value' of a thing is neither the price paid for it, nor the amount of present satisfaction

* *Unto this Last*, p. 156.

it yields to the consumer, but the intrinsic service it is capable of yielding by its right use. Of commercial goods, or any other class of goods, those which have a capacity for satisfying wholesome human wants are 'wealth,' those which pander to some base or injurious desire of man are not wealth, but 'illth,' availing as they do, not for life but for death. Thus he (Ruskin) posits as the starting-point of Political Economy a standard of life not based upon present subjective valuations of 'consumers,' but upon eternal and immutable principles of health and disease, justice and injustice.''*

In *Unto this Last* it sometimes appears that Ruskin refused to recognize that political economy was capable of being made a study distinct from the wider study of the art of life which would include all sorts of human activities that yield vital value. But in *Munera Pulveris* he virtually confines his analysis to the production and consumption of economic ''goods'' which come within the compass of ''cost'' and ''utility.'' His central thought is the development of ''value'' in the sense of that which ''avails'' towards life. And here he distinguishes what he terms ''intrinsic'' from ''effectual'' value. '' 'Intrinsic' value is the absolute power to support life. A sheaf of wheat of given quality and weight has in it a measurable power of sustaining the substance of the body; a cubic foot of pure air, a fixed power of sustaining its warmth;

* Page 79.

and a cluster of flowers of given beauty a fixed power of enlivening or animating the senses and heart.'' But whether any particular object will yield such a service depends upon the state of the recipient, ''his capacity to use it.'' Wealth has no effectual value if there is no capacity to use it in the recipient. Its effectual value increases with the capacity of the user. The finest picture in the world has no effectual value if there is nobody available to appreciate its beauty. Even ''a sheaf of wheat'' may be devoid of ''effectual'' value if its owner has a surfeit, and it cannot pass to another who is in need of food. Curiously enough this view of wealth and value is here confined to the human utility of articles of wealth and takes no direct account of their human cost. This is the stranger inasmuch as Ruskin's earliest and strongest charge against the economic system was that, by dividing and mechanizing labour, it took away all interest in and joy of work. He was artist before he became economist, and it was the vital cost of excessive and degraded work that drew him into his passionate campaign. But though in *Munera Pulveris* he appears to concentrate upon utility in its sense of humanly serviceable consumption as his central theme, his wider economic thesis lies in the correlation of human cost to human utility. A subdivided routine-producer could not be an efficient consumer of any of the more worthy sorts of wealth. Nor could an idle consumer, living not by his labour but on his ''means.''

Though Ruskin in no single book set out his economic "science" in its full strength, a reading of his several writings yields a sufficient basis for a human political economy, which should take account of the related processes of production and consumption and should evaluate both processes in terms of human worth.

From him I drew the basic thought for my subsequent economic writings, viz. the necessity of going behind the current monetary estimates of wealth, cost, and utility, to reach the body of human benefits and satisfactions which gave them a real meaning. But it is one thing to judge that all costs of production and utilization of consumption should be expressed in terms of human satisfaction and quite another thing to formulate such a judgment. Several sorts of difficulty at once become apparent. In this "human" economics it is almost impossible to differentiate the satisfaction and dissatisfaction one calls "economic" from other vital goods and ills which lie outside this economic ambit. That is to say, there is the tendency to fuse economic with other vital processes so as to disable them for separate study. Next there is the question how far one can take as criteria of human value the actual satisfactions and dissatisfactions currently attributed to various acts of production and consumption or should insist upon reference to what Ruskin termed their "'intrinsic' values." Lastly, there remains the question how far the pleasures and pains of one man can be compared with those of another.

I cite these difficulties here, not with a view of presenting ready solutions, but because they affect the substance of nearly all my later thought and writing. I did not even grasp them in their full significance at the time, and they proved to be sources of some confusion when I came to formulate my economics in terms of "human value." In the nineties my mind was fumbling after the conception and expression of an economics which was more art than science, and, therefore, more qualitative than quantitative in its estimate of value, wealth, cost, and utility. But the full significance of this revolt against a distinctively quantitative science did not emerge until a good deal later.

For while I was engaged in the Ruskinian service, I also occupied myself in the more definitely economic task of an analysis of the different sorts and conditions of bargain and marketing by which the distribution or apportionment of wealth among the owners of the several factors of production took place. This was the beginning of my various endeavours to express intelligibly my growing realization of the injustice, inhumanity, and waste in those processes of price-fixing which determined the respective payments made to landowners, capitalists, employers, and the various classes of workers. What first prompted me to this endeavour was my sense of the unsatisfactory way in which economists found separate ''laws'' to express rent, interest, profit, wages. In actual economic processes all the factors of production were required to co-operate, and that co-operation was an organic process which precluded the separate assignment of any part of the products to any one of them. Different kinds and quantities of land, capital, labour were needed for each of these acts of co-operative production. The calculation of how much of each factor was required in a given business was based on the conception of a factory, a workshop, or a retail store regarded as an organic whole.

In considering the parts played by the several sorts of land, capital, and labour, it seemed, however, necessary to attribute to them for their several units a measurable amount of productive utility for the various uses to which they might be put. Here I found that little had been done towards such measurement except in the case of land, and that even there the tendency had been to treat all land as if it were the same sort of stuff differing only in the degree of fertility for a single purpose. There was ''marginal'' land, just worth cultivation on a no-rent or nominal rent basis, and better acres paid a ''differential'' rent, measuring the superiority of their yield over that of the marginal land. The dictum, that ''rent'' did not ''enter into'' cost of production and price, was based on this quite unwarranted assumption of a no-rent margin. For as soon as it was realized that there were several alternative uses for a piece of land, it became evident that only the lowest of these uses yielded no rent at the margin. The worst hop-land paid a positive rent, the worst market-garden land, the worst building land, because the worst acre for any of these purposes was not "marginal" for wheat growing, pasture, or some other alternative use from which it was diverted.

This reflection made it obvious that "land" did not differ from capital and labour as regards price and productivity. There existed in any productive community capital, in the sense of plant, raw materials, etc., which was inferior to other capital, and was only just worth using at any particular time if its service could be purchased at a nominal price, just covering cost of maintenance or of replacement. So likewise with the labour available at any given time for some particular purpose: it varied in quality or efficiency and the least efficient worker only got a bare subsistence wage. The more efficient plant and labour got payments corresponding to their superiority over the "marginal" plant and labour. My mind, working along this comparison, sought to grade all the factors of production according to their degrees of efficiency, and to apply to industry in general the law of differential rents and of margins. Payments out of the price of the ultimate products thus emerged under several heads, applicable to each of the factors: first, costs of maintenance or replacement, applicable to land as to capital and labour; secondly, marginal or minimum payments to the owners of the least efficient of the several factors in employment; finally, differential payments due to the owners of super-marginal factors.

This analysis conducted so far appears to assume the necessity and even the equity of the current economic system (save for the element of land rents). The owners of capital and labour who take super-marginal payments may be held to get them in virtue of the higher personal effort and efficiency in putting their "savings," brains, and labour-power to the best uses. Thus we get a justification of the competitive *laisser-faire* economy.

But further reflection showed me that two false assumptions underlay this view, one that all units of production were infinitely divisible in quantity, and, secondly, that they enjoyed equal opportunities for entering any market for their employment.

The failure to fulfil those two conditions is, however, manifest. Units of capital and of labour are not infinitely divisible. In any given manufacturing business the minimum unit of real capital may be the whole plant of a mill, or, at any rate, one expensive machine: the unit of labour is for most purposes the week's employment of a worker's time. Nor can new savings flow freely into all sorts of investment, distributing themselves accurately in accordance with their most productive use. Most remunerative uses are safeguarded for capitalists in control, or are only open to certain orders of investors. Human labour cannot, it is notorious, have full knowledge of and free access to all sorts of work, from the work of research and invention, or of business control, to the various grades of mental and manual skilled and unskilled labour.

It was the nature of this unfreedom and inequality in the competitive conditions which led me in the later nineties into my early challenge of the equity of the distribution of incomes. I then set myself to examine the actual operations of the owners of supply and demand, as expressed in the bargaining that determined those market prices which are the main instruments for the distribution of incomes. From this examination there emerged two salient truths: first, that in many markets the volume of supply was restricted, naturally or artificially, so as to give to the sellers, as a body, a superior bargaining force for the sale of their goods, reflected in a higher price than was economically necessary to evoke their productive services. Secondly, the selling prices, even where "free bargaining" prevailed, were determined in accord with the relative importance to certain buyers or sellers of effecting a purchase or sale: these marginal buyers or sellers fixed the price at a point where it was just worth their while to buy or sell, the other buyers or sellers got from this price something more than would have been a sufficient inducement, i.e. a "surplus" element. This "surplus," corresponding to differential rent for land, had no rational or equitable basis: it was an element of "unreason" permeating the bargaining process in all markets, either for consumption goods, production goods, or productive services.

The crude and commonly accepted notion that the general result of the current competitive system was to place the benefits of competition in the hands of "the consumer," and that, since everybody is a consumer, all improvements of productivity ultimately benefited consumers as a body, was thus put into the scrap-heap, and there began to emerge the view that economic "force" was a main determinant in the distribution of wealth. This argument in its entirety was set out in my book *The Economics of Distribution*, published in 1900 by The Macmillan Company of New York. This publication was unfortunate, in so much as it reached few English readers and was scarcely noticed in English reviews.

There was little attempt at the time to associate the definitely humanist and ethical trend of my Ruskinian thought with this analysis of the economic processes of distribution. It was not until a later period that the two trends of thought were correlated. This postponement was partly due to the absorption of much of my time and energy in movements and events which brought me into touch with the more active reformers of the nineties.

CHAPTER IV

CONTACTS WITH POLITICAL AND ETHICAL MOVEMENTS

THOUGH I had never become a full-blooded rationalist in the sense of holding that reasoning was the sole method of attaining truth and of assessing values, my mind had long been set in that direction, and when I came to London I soon found myself consorting with persons who had shed theology and who sought to apply rationalism in the fields of ethics and politics. One of my earliest and most intimate associates was Bradlaugh's chief intellectual lieutenant, J. M. Robertson, who was assistant editor of the *National Reformer*, which took for its leading tenets Atheism, Republicanism, and Birth Control. Equipped with unrivalled powers of controversy, immense industry in the acquisition of knowledge in history, science, and philosophy, and a wonderfully accurate and ready memory, he devoted the greater part of his life to the history and the current practice of free-thought. Though later on in the early twentieth century he was drawn into active participation in the Free Trade controversy, was elected into Parliament and even held office as Under-Secretary in the Board of Trade, his heart never lay in politics. He could never become a sound party man, for, though certain early excesses of the rising Labour movement repelled him and drove him into the Liberal camp, he was never quite at ease there and was, I think, glad to return to his books and his controversial theories. When I knew him best, in the nineties, the virtues and at least one curious defect were exceedingly impressive upon one in general sympathy with his rationalism in all fields of its application. The defect was an excessive combativeness which was apt to pursue every detected falsehood or fallacy to its remotest origins and a related failure to assign the proper scale of importance to the several errors of his "enemies." I remember on one occasion venturing to protest against the ferocity of some indictment, and he answered: "You forget that I am only four generations from a painted Pict." It would be wrong, however, to neglect in any estimate of Robertson, the intense "humanism" which underlay his "spirit of revolt" against the popular creeds of his day and of the past. In personal intercourse he showed a most kindly disposition in all the ordinary affairs of life. It was only when our conversation brought up some controversial topic of the day that the fighting temper was aroused. How far my association with this remarkable man influenced my mind and lines of thought I cannot judge. It certainly strengthened my anti-religious bent and clarified the doctrine of "determinism" which at that time threatened to dominate my outlook in all fields of activity. But though we first met in the adoption of a common economic heresy, "Over-saving," as my economic studies led me along the Labour and Socialist paths, Robertson stood upon the whole by *laisser-faire* Liberalism, and a gradual breach came into our politics and economics.

It may seem at first sight rather difficult to link up the Scot J. M. Robertson with another Scot, Ramsay MacDonald, with whom I had a close personal contact during the same period. Both were men of fine presence and of imposing personality. MacDonald came into my life a year or two later than Robertson, as I remember from a remark made by a German governess, who spoke of MacDonald as "die zweite Schönheit." A Labour Party was not then in being, the I.L.P. had not yet entered Parliament, and MacDonald's earliest standing was that of an independent radical with Socialist sympathies. My relations with him took on a more impersonal form when we became associated in the production of a magazine entitled the *Progressive Review*, which ran a brief precarious life from 1896 to 1898. The title chosen for this magazine, taken in conjunction with the names of its chief supporters, editors, and writers, is an indication of the new alignment in the field of politics due to the intrusion of important economic issues which had long been waiting in the political background. William Clarke, then a writer for the *Daily Chronicle* and a member of the Fabian Executive, was the active editor, to whom I rendered such assistance as I could, while Ramsay MacDonald was secretary, and Herbert Samuel an active worker and supporter, with Charles Trevelyan and Richard Stapley aiding and abetting in the enterprise. Samuel I first came into contact with when, as a candidate for one of the Oxfordshire Divisions, he was giving his attention to projects of land reform, and generally preparing himself for the active political career of after years. His close friend, Trevelyan, was then not a Labour man or a Socialist in any declared sense. The *Progressive Review* was definitely opposed to such a general Socialist policy as Keir Hardie was allowed to advocate in one of its early numbers. The term "New Liberalism" was adopted by Samuel and others as rightly descriptive of its aims. That "New" Liberalism differed from the old in that it envisaged more clearly the need for important economic reforms, aiming to give a positive significance to the "equality" which figured in the democratic triad of liberty, equality, fraternity. "A many-sided policy of thorough economic reform" was the task confronting Parliament as Samuel saw it in 1896. Or, if we turn from "equality" to "liberty," we may take as its aim the passage quoted by Haldane from T. H. Green in the second number of the *Review*. "When we measure the progress of a society by its growth in freedom, we measure it by the increasing development and exercise on the whole of those powers of contributing to social good with which we believe the members of the society to be endowed; in short, by the greater power of the citizens as a body to make the most and best of themselves.''*

But though ''the citizens as a body'' must utilize the State as their main political instrument for the promotion of this ''social good,'' the editorial policy of the *Review* was keenly alive to the dangers of a powerful State, taken as an instrument of absolute control and adducing ''Reasons of State'' as an overruling principle of policy. One of the last articles in the *Review* was a strong endorsement of a protest by John Morley against the reincarnation of Machiavellism, especially in Germany. The writer, moreover, points out that Imperialism, as practised on the Congo, in Matabeleland, and elsewhere, works along the same evil assumption that ''Human claims, universal morality, mercy, justice, pity, all count for nothing in the minds of those who mainly administer affairs, when weighed in the balance against State interests.''

The growing ''Imperialism'' and the growing ''Socialism'' exhibit the same danger of an absolute State control. ''In the light of this idea, that the State exists for the individual, not the individual for the State, all existing institutions must be tried, and they will stand or fall according as they can bear the searching test.†

Taken by itself, this statement may seem to resolve all ''social good'' into the good of the individuals

* Page 136.

† The *Progressive Review*, p. 293.

who compose society. This was not, however, the intention of the writer, for he adduces "the general will" as a spiritual reality, organic in character, and operative through the State, as through other organs of co-operation. We had here in the *Review* a first serious attempt to draw the attention, not of a few intellectuals but of a wider thinking minority of citizens, to the difficulties besetting the intrusion of the State, whether autocratic or democratic, into new economic spheres of activity. Another article, "Is Democracy a Failure?" directly confronts those difficulties which now, forty years later, figure in the forefront of political history.

But it was distinctive of the *Progressive Review* that, though primarily political-economic in its outlook, it realized that "progress" was "cultural" in the widest human sense. Not a few of its articles were written by leaders of free-thought in the fields of art and literature. Havelock Ellis, Edward Carpenter, William Archer, James Oliphant, Karl Blind, are among the names recorded. The early collapse of this *Review* was, I think, a great misfortune. Had it lived, it might have had a most useful influence in moulding the thought, policy, and structure of the new Labour-Socialist Party which was just beginning to emerge from the clouded counsels and mixed interests of diverse "progressive" movements. It was, however, the usual race between a slow-growing circulation and limited finance which has brought to an end so many promising literary projects—one aspect of an economic determinism sharpened by a secret recognition that our sense of "progress" involved peril to the purse, power, and prestige of the ruling classes in business, politics, society.

For myself, I think the many contacts which my work on the *Review* brought with more mature minds than my own, and in particular the experience of the intricate interactions in the worlds of thought and action, were of immense value in widening and deepening my outlook. It became impossible for me to devote myself to an arid economic science which boasted its growing exactitude and took "the measuring rod of money" as its final criterion of value.

Other associations belonging to this period of the nineties ministered to the same tendency, the close relations between economics and politics and the search after a social ethics which should harmonize the two and bring them both under a broader concept of the art of human welfare.

Here it behoves me to say something about the Ethical Movement which began its enlarged activities in the nineties. Soon after I came to London in the late eighties I found that my work in University Extension brought me into touch with the London Ethical Society, of which J. H. Muirhead and Bernard Bosanquet were active leaders. In substance it was an attempt of a few Oxford philosophers, not content with the seclusion of an academic life, to furnish thought and leadership to movements "for the amelioration of the condition of the working classes." The men I have named, with a few others, had been associated with the Charity Organisation Society, a creation of the late seventies, which vested its reforms in the improvement of the character of the workers. But it became evident that any wider reforms of working-class character demanded a prior process of moral instruction for the upper and middle classes who had hitherto taken their social creed and charitable policy from the Orthodox Churches. Our ethical leaders rightly emphasized the need of a reasonable social and personal ethics, based not on any theology but upon a rational conception of moral welfare and applied to working out the conditions of "the good life." My experience of this Ethical Society led me to regard it as excellent in its assertion of free discussion, but as committed so strongly to the stress on individual moral character, as the basis of social progress, as to make it the enemy of that political-economic democracy which I was coming to regard as the chief instrument of social progress and justice. This moral individualism was not, however, equally developed in the other ethical societies which were coming into existence at the close of the century. Nor was it applicable to the earliest Ethical Society, that of South Place, which from the time of Charles James Fox, the Corn Law reformer, had been a centre of free-thought and free speech on all the controversial issues of the age. Unitarian in its origin, it retained the name of a "religious" society after Moncure Conway, its American re-founder, became its minister. The term "ethical" was introduced when Dr. Coit took charge in 1888. Though problems of economic reform did not take concrete shape under Conway, the ethics of social responsibility figured largely in his teaching. My own personal association with South Place dated from 1897, and two years later I became one of its regular lecturers, figuring as a sort of middle-man between J. M. Robertson and Herbert Burrows, a committed Socialist. The wide divergence of our views on many matters made no difficulty before an audience that prided itself upon an "open mind." A test of this liberty of speech was afforded me when the South African War occupied the national mind at the close of the century. Though the sympathies of prominent members of South Place were sharply divided on the merits of the war, no attempt was made to "boycott" the strong pro-Boer utterances made from the platform by the lecturers, who were in agreement in their condemnation of this brutal piece of Imperialism.

My close connection with this liberal platform, lasting continuously for thirty-six years, was of great help to me in clarifying my thought and enlarging my range of interests in matters of social conduct. Addressing audiences consisting for the most part of men and women of the business and professional classes, with a scattering of educated clerks and manual workers, I found myself driven to put ethical significance into a variety of current topics and events, many of which belonged to the fields of politics and economics. But I had first to make up my own mind, before communicating the result to others. Though such a fragmentary process had its defects, it served on the whole to bring together what at first sight seemed widely sundered pieces of thought and valuation, and so to give an increasing measure of cohesion to the deeper process of intellectual order needed to carry out the humanization of economic thinking which I had taken as my primary intellectual task.

CHAPTER V

SOUTH AFRICAN AND AMERICAN STUDIES

THE Boer War was both a turning-point in my career and an illumination to my understanding of the real relations between economics and politics which were to occupy so large a place in my future work. The persistent opportunist pressures by which our wide-spread Empire had grown up and the relative parts played in the process by political ambitions and commercial gains had become a matter of close attention since Lord Beaconsfield had organized the Prince of Wales's visit to India and had staged the magnificent imperial parades at Queen Victoria's two Jubilees. The conscious pride in our Empire had become a new and potent factor in our national sentiment and was beginning to evoke some envy and criticism in foreign quarters. Mark Twain, watching the Jubilee procession, remarked that "The English are mentioned in Holy Scripture—'Blessed are the meek for they shall inherit the earth.' " So long as our colonial possessions, a quarter of the globe, were free to the trade and the migration of other nations, no active sense of grievance was evoked. But when Joseph Chamberlain set out to convert the Empire into a close preserve by his policy of tariffs and preferences, and the magnificent projects of Cecil Rhodes began to influence the mind and language of English politicians, the larger significance of our Imperialism became manifest. The procedure was unhappily dramatized in the Jameson raid and in the revelations of our public inquiry which indicated the connivance of important British Statesmen in this attempt at forcible aggression. The outbreak of the Boer War in 1899 will, however, rank in history as the simplest and plainest example of the interplay of political and economic motives in Imperialism. For the political ambitions of Chamberlain, Milner, and Rhodes were consciously and skilfully utilized by the mine-owners of the Rand for their purpose of profitable control. The mixed Outlanders in the Transvaal demanded that British force should be applied, so as to relieve them from the taxation and other interferences of the Kruger government, and put them in the necessary political control of the country.

What was my particular personal concern in this affair? I happened to have written in the *Contemporary Review* of March 1899 an article on "Imperialism," containing some references to the recent history of South Africa, which came before the eyes of L. T. Hobhouse, then the chief political leader-writer for the *Manchester Guardian*. Hobhouse, destined to become one of my closest friends and associates in many other projects, urged his Editor, C. P. Scott, to send me out on a voyage of political inquiry to South Africa when the outlook began to be dangerous.

Though I had had no experience in newspaper work, except as an occasional reviewer, I seized the opportunity to see the working of Imperialism at close quarters, and after several talks with Scott and Hobhouse launched upon what was for me a novel adventure. I met and talked with all the leading public men, Kruger, Reitz, Smuts, and Hertzog in the Transvaal and the Free State; Milner, Schreiner, Merriman, Sauer, Hofmeyr, at the Cape; I dined with Rhodes at Groot Schuur on the eve of the outbreak of war, and busied myself to learn all I could about the division between Dutch and British sentiments in the Colony. While Milner told me that it was necessary "to break the dominion of Africanderdom," Rhodes professed to disbelieve in the Boers' willingness to fight, and even when the war began the situation in Cape Colony remained for some time doubtful. The lesson I learned from this experience was the dominant power of a particularly crude form of capitalism operating in a mixed political field. It became evident that, while the politicians were hesitant and divided, the capitalists of the Rand were planning straight for war and were using the British Press of South Africa as their instrument for rousing the war-spirit in England. Though the large number of interested English investors in South African mines formed the nucleus of their appeal, they were well aware that England would need to visualize the war in terms of morals and humanity. So for some months their Press was turned upon outrages upon Outlanders in Johannesburg, while missionary opinion was mobilized to denounce the cruelties practised by the Boers upon the native population in South Africa. The diplomatic story of Outlander grievances, foisted on our public from diplomatic sources, was wildly exaggerated. Living for several weeks in Johannesburg at the very time of these alleged disorders, I experienced no personal difficulties and, though the timidest of God's creatures, I felt no fear in moving about the streets at night. Though a few acts of violence were committed, there was no campaign of violence, and it became clear to me that, if Smuts and Schreiner had had the conduct of the Bloemfontein Conference in their hands, instead of Kruger and Milner, there would have been no war, in spite of the goadings of a "kept" Press. War came from the joint drive of capitalism in South Africa and the new imperalism in England.

This experience had two effects upon my life. It gave realistic support to economic opinions derived in the main from theoretic interpretations of history, and it plunged me for some years into the heated atmosphere of political controversy. Returning to England shortly after the outbreak of war, I cast the articles written for the *Manchester Guardian*, with some other material, into a book entitled *The South African War*, followed in 1901 by an analysis of the modern war-spirit called *The Psychology of Jingoism*, which dwelt upon the mixture of national arrogance and folly at the disposal of the imperialists and business men who were the working partners in the preparation and production of modern wars. A larger volume, *Imperialism*, published in 1902,* contained a fuller and more formal discussion of the same theme, dwelling in more detail upon the economic causation and linking the rising struggle for empire with the pressure for investment of surplus profits in the development of backward countries.

During those years I was drawn away from my studies of the history and theory of capitalist economy into controversial causes and movements, which, though not unrelated to my earlier positions, were evidently removed from the calm, dispassionate atmosphere which economic scientists professed and sometimes practised. I cannot pretend that this latter process was favourable to a disinterested and purely objective view of economic science. On the contrary, by enlisting my combative instincts in defence of my heretical views of capitalism as the source of unjust distribution, over-saving, and an economic impulsion to adventurous imperialism, it led me for a time to an excessive and too simple advocacy of the economic determination of history. When I wrote my volume on *Imperialism* I had not yet gathered into clear perspective the nature of the interaction between economics, politics, and ethics, needed for anyone

* Reissued by George Allen & Unwin, Ltd., in 1938.

who might wish to claim the title of Sociologist. It was only at this period, when I was entering middle age, that I became largely engaged in active movements and "causes" along these three related lines. As lecturer for ethical societies, controversial anti-Imperialist and semi-Socialist in the Press, and sometimes on the platform, I gradually brought my ethical and political thoughts and sentiments into what I still hold to be their true organic relations with the business life and its economic science. "Economics" still remained the central occupation of my mind, but I was more and more drawn into the two positions which severed me from economic orthodoxy, first the insistence upon the growing part to be played by the State and political forces in the realities of economic life; secondly, the fundamental "immorality" of a business system in which all markets were morally damaged by differences in bargaining power and the settlement of market prices alike for goods and services by the play of selfish interests.

A more salutary experience of this period was the series of long visits to the United States and Canada, where I came into close contact with a play of economic forces simpler and more dramatic than those operative in England. A long journey through Canada in the autumn of 1905, recorded in a series of articles in the *Daily Chronicle* and afterwards in a small book *Canada To-day*,* gave me new light on the relations between

* London: T. Fisher Unwin.

economics and politics within the British Empire. In particular it disclosed the beginnings of imperial protectionism in the Preferences which had begun to operate in 1898. The general course of Canadian trade during subsequent years showed that, while the tariff had checked the pace of the decline which had been taking place in British imports, it had not stopped that decline, and that the general course of Canadian trade, both import and export, was flowing more strongly than ever towards the United States. This was only natural, because in many classes of raw materials and foodstuffs the United States had a virtual monopoly of the import market, while many of the special needs and tastes of Canadian consumers could only be supplied from American sources. Moreover, there was no intention in Canada to allow impediments to be placed in the development of her own rising manufactures by allowing the free competition either of British or American imports. Neither the theory nor the policy of Free Trade had any hold upon the politicians or business men of Canada, or of the other Dominions, which later came into the preferential ring. An absolute monopoly of the home market for the home producer was their fixed creed. How to reconcile this prevailing motive with a favourable market for Empire goods which lay outside home production without damaging their trade relations, import and export, with foreign neighbours, has been a problem of increasing complexity.

Contact with this problem in its early shape brought into clear sight the connection between Imperialism and Protectionism which Chamberlain developed in his later career. Both these "isms" received strong support from the "forced" export policy which comes from over-saving and the urgent need for foreign markets to supplement the deficiency of the home market. This deficiency, due to insufficient income of the working classes, was seen to be directly responsible for the "slump" in each trade cycle. In a general time of "unemployment" for our capital and labour, a tariff that will keep out foreign competing goods from our market has an arguable case. If we have idle plant and labour in the motor-car industry, a tariff which will induce purchasers of cars to buy English-made cars, instead of American or French, will increase the total volume of employment in this country, provided the increased price of motor cars is not so high as to cause an equivalent loss of purchasing power for other commodities. A fall in exports will naturally follow any such reduction of imports, but the English-made cars will, through ordinary monetary operations, exchange against other English goods somewhat larger in amount than those which would have gone out in export payment. The net result would be a larger volume of production and employment in this country, at the expense of production and employment in other countries suffering from unemployment. It is a selfish and indeed a short-sighted policy, for when trade "recovery" has taken place we shall find ourselves hampered by tariffs which are obstructive to the best use of our productive resources but which have become vested interests and difficult to remove. Along this line of imperialist protection I thus found further support for my over-saving heresy.

My American experiences brought other aspects of capitalism to the front. Though the lecture tours which I made in the East and Middle West of the United States were chiefly to Universities, other contacts with business men's and women's clubs and more popular audiences gave me a clearer understanding of the blend of ruthless competition and equally ruthless monopoly which characterized the economic and political scene in America. I saw a business system which had grown up under free competition and equality of opportunity passing into trusts and other combines derived from the acquisition of lands containing the best supplies of coal, iron, oil, and other important raw materials, supported by railroad and banking connections and by tariffs directed against outside competition. Not less significant were the private ownership and control by a few strong business men in the old cities of the East and the new rising cities of the Middle West over the profitable supply of public utilities and the growing land values. The first clear and comprehensive exposure of the corruption of democratic institutions in American

States and cities was given by Ostrogorski in his *Democracy* (1912), where the operations of the party and electoral system in the hands of business interests were set forth with an abundance of detailed evidence that was convincing. The early history of the Standard Oil Trust, by my friend Henry D. Lloyd of Chicago, accompanied by Lincoln Steffens's *The Shame of the Cities*, helped to reveal those weaknesses in American institutions, and my personal talks with these and other "muck-rakers" (as they were termed by the Press of the profiteers) gave me a clearer understanding of the defects of a political democracy divorced from the terms of economic equality that are essential to its equitable working.

Repeated visits to America during the past half-century have perhaps taught me more of the ethics and politics of the economic system in its modern capitalistic shape and development than any experience available in England, where the play of social-economic forces is more obscure and more impeded by traditional and humane considerations. This contrast appears most striking in the recent American efforts to achieve the elements of political control over unemployment, destitution, and conditions of labour, which have long been established as accepted factors in the working of our own economic system.

Before leaving the American scene I should acknowledge the deep debt I owe to several economic and political teachers with whom I was brought into close contact. One of my early American friends was John Graham Brooks, who for many years was the chief interpreter of current European affairs to American audiences and the closest student of new American movements. Though his sympathies were exceedingly liberal, he owed much of his influence to a careful adhesion to a descriptive factual method of address which enabled him to keep on easy terms of communication with all sorts and conditions of men. Professor E. A. Ross, one of the foremost sociologists, also helped me towards a clearer understanding of American affairs, when I spent a fortnight with him on a lecture visit to Wisconsin. He and Veblen (of whom I shall speak later) seemed to me to have the most comprehensive understanding of the recent evolution of American political-economic life. Incidentally, my visit to Madison gave me an interesting light upon a type of political leader whose mentality would have been impossible in any European country. Madison was the "home town" of William Jennings Bryan, whose rhetorical campaign on the Silver question brought him within sight of the Presidency. As he drove me about the country in his "buggy" he dilated upon the advantages of the scrapping of officials with every change of party, because it brought new men with new experiences into office. The idea that new officials might not be as good as experienced office holders never occurred to him. Every American could easily adapt himself to any post to which, for party reasons, he was appointed! When I met him later in England, after years of further campaigning all over the States, I found the same simple, honest, fervent nature, decorated with the same power of empty oratory.

If, as is likely, these vivid experiences tended to over-stress my sense of the dangers of a dominant capitalism, this bias was to some extent offset by other travels into more peaceful countries. In 1902 I spent a pleasant, profitable fortnight in Denmark with Seebohm Rowntree, who was making a study of the "milk" problem, and there learned a good deal about the education and politics of what is perhaps the most genuinely civilized country in the world. Four years later I spent several weeks in Switzerland, investigating the operations of the Referendum and the general working of Swiss democracy, in order to complete the work to which my friend H. D. Lloyd had given so much attention shortly before his death. The distinctive thought that emerged from these visits was the advantage which a small nation, living upon an equalitarian level in its business and social relations, enjoyed in the working of democracy.

These travels, bringing me into close contact with practical affairs in various countries, strengthened my distinctive attitude in social thinking, viz. the testing of all political and economic conduct by the criteria of human welfare, however difficult and imperfect that process may be regarded from any standpoint of scientific exactitude.

CHAPTER VI

THE RISE OF SOCIOLOGY IN ENGLAND

I HAVE dwelt at so much length upon the conditions of America and other foreign countries which influenced my economic thinking as to obscure the far greater importance of my knowledge of English conditions. It is sometimes urged that a serious student of our economic system ought to obtain direct personal experience in a number of focal situations. He should serve in a textile factory, on a railway, a farm, should hold a post in a bank or a city office, a wholesale and retail store, so as to have real understanding of the business terms and facts he has to handle as economist. Though such varied experience is perhaps impossible, much of the best recent economic thinking undoubtedly has come from men who have served in business or official capacities that have brought them into close contact with detailed realities of economic life. While there is, of course, some danger of such specialism disabling one from seeing the forest as a whole, some direct personal contact with material processes of production is an immense advantage to one who can escape this danger. Though I never had this advantage, my work lying in the teaching and literary world, I seized what opportunities lay in my path for getting glimpses of our national industries,

During the nineties, and even later, my lectures on Problems of Poverty and related themes brought me into contact with a good many business men and trade unionists who were willing to show me the works in which they were engaged. Even such fragmentary contacts with industrial realities were of great service in correcting my jejune generalizations. Later on some work of investigation done for the Board of Trade, and service on several public committees, including the important one presided over by Lord Colwyn, helped me a good deal to adjust my ideas to authentic facts and established situations. I am aware how slight and haphazard such personal experience has been, as compared with that of a regular worker or employer. But it did help me to a better understanding of the producer side of the economic problem. On the consumer side everybody with a limited income and many needs is compelled to be a more or less skilled amateur: the only experts are the social workers who study closely working-class expenditure on a sufficient scale. Though my heresies have led me to assign supreme significance to the financial situation of the consumer, I cannot pretend to possess intimate knowledge of anybody else's standard of consumption, and living, as I have done for the most part upon the least defensible of all forms of unearned income, I have not been driven to the nice calculations of expenditure to which most men with families to keep are driven.

This last consideration, carrying as it does a natural bias in favour of a system retaining opportunities of unearned income, may have influenced my economic thinking in one or more of several ways. With a high value for security I may have been led to a half-conscious defence of "securities" as a mainstay of a sound economic system. Or, conscious of this bias, I may have brought an excessive weight of counter-bias in order to assert my independence of thought. There is also a third possibility open to one who realizes the manifold injustices of the capitalist system, viz. to propound a remedy so drastic that there is little or no danger of its adoption in our lifetime. When George Bernard Shaw argues in favour of an absolute equalization of income, as he does in his *Intelligent Woman's Guide to Socialism*,* he leaves himself open to the retort that he must know quite well that such a condition precludes any effective interference with his own large body of wealth. Fourthly, the fact that unearned income enabled me to devote most of my time and energy to the unremunerative work of writing economic books, though not formally accepted as a justification of such income, must often have presented itself in the light of an extenuating circumstance. It is, indeed, offered by many "intellectuals" as a complete defence of such unearned wealth as provides the requisite freedom to do the best kinds of work. Thus there are so many snares that no man, however

* London: Constable.

reasonable and disinterested he may think himself to be, can be sure he is evading all of them. The psychology of a situation where one's own personal interests stand in sharp opposition to one's cherished intellectual code carries possibilities of tragic or of comic error. It is evidently impossible for me to carry further this analysis, though it was necessary in order to present the proper limitations to my "objective" thinking.

This attitude of detachment was strengthened by my virtual abandonment of University Extension work in the beginning of the new century and the devotion of most of my energy towards articles and books developing my welfare economics. Most of the articles written for the *Manchester Guardian* and the *Speaker* had a political import such as Free Trade, the Referendum, Imperial Expansion. But, as already indicated, here as in my published books, ethics in the sense of human valuations was continually asserting its sway over economics and politics. This trinity of forces did not, however, imply the acceptance of any absolute conception of "the good life" such as ethical teachers have sometimes seemed to claim. For the substance of "welfare" itself must shift with the changes that take place in economic and political institutions and activities. This dynamic conception of welfare, while precluding a separate monetary or other economic criterion, demands that economic activities shall be brought continually into conformity with the new and more enlightened conceptions of welfare.

This signifies a conception of social evolution, family, tribal, national, cosmopolitan, in which ethics, politics, and economics play their respective inter-related parts. So we seem to pass into the intellectual realm of sociology. Now sociology, connected with the names of Comte and Herbert Spencer, had not yet won in this country, or anywhere save in America, any firm acceptance as a science. When a society of sociology was first founded here in the beginning of this century by the efforts of Patrick Geddes, Victor Branford, and a few other active thinkers, it seemed to many of us a precarious project, partly because it appeared to conflict with the tendency to specialize and subdivide which the conception of "thoroughness" involved. But this was not the only difficulty. The men I have named had committed themselves more closely to the Le Play interpretation of social evolution in terms of Place, Work, and Folk than others, even among those who welcomed the formation of the new organization, were willing to go. This was especially applicable to L. T. Hobhouse who, though rendering active help in forming the Society, regarded as somewhat strained and even fantastic some of the positions and terminology of the Le Play School. Though various scientific studies of social activities and institutions, such as comparative religion, mythology, law, morality, had been emerging in the late nineteenth century, little had been done to link them into what could be termed a social science, a study of society as an evolving unitary system. Hobhouse, setting himself to this task, brought the necessary equipment of a philosopher, with the conception of progressive human values which cannot be got from a purely inductive study of human activities and institutions, but is yet essential to give human meaning to social progress. Professor Ginsberg states the problem in the following lucid terms. "The scientific problem is to correlate the several aspects of social change and to measure the kind and amount of growth in the light of criteria not necessarily ethical but analogous to those that might be employed by the biologist in dealing with organic evolution. The ethical problem is to determine whether the development thus established, if it be established, satisfies ethical standards of value. The former type of investigation leads to a comparative study of culture deriving its data from anthropology and history, and seeks to discover whether there is a thread of continuity running through the tangle of the countless processes convergent and divergent which make up the life of man on earth. The other presupposes an ethical theory and a method of applying ethical criteria to the phases of historical development."*

Progress of personality as a harmonious development

* L. T. Hobhouse, p. 125.

of the interplay of individual and social motives was the key to the social thinking of Hobhouse. His stress on personality as the end and object of all social processes carried a denial of any group or social mind other than the orderly interplay of individual minds and reduced such a term as "esprit de corps" to a personal feeling common to the members of a cooperative group. To him there was nothing possible or desirable for man in the communism of a beehive or an anthill where the individual welfare of the several members was subordinated to, controlled by, and consisted of the general welfare of a social organism. In any human society evolving into such an organism, the whole value of free personality would be lost.

Though Hobhouse, of course, fully admitted the effects of social institutions and intercourse in helping to mould the character of a person, nobody in close acquaintance with him could fail to perceive that his will-power for self-determination in all affairs down to the smallest home detail was unusually strong, and that while freely expending his energy for his own conception of the good of others, he did not easily yield to the efforts of others to influence his line of conduct. This supremacy of a personal rational will over all the impulses and emotions which seek their separate expression was the core not only of his thinking but of his feeling. Its validity is not impaired by the special force of his personal psychical make-up, but the latter must certainly be taken into account in regarding his thought. Few personalities were so strong and rigorous in their central rationality, a command which belittles alike the play of the fragmentary selves, so apparent in the lives of ordinary men, and the merging of personalities in easy companionship or close co-operation. One other feature of his social philosophy has sometimes been called in question, his presentation of supreme personal value in terms of harmony. That there must be a measure of harmonious co-operation in all personal or social progress is certain, but the achievement of complete harmony would seem to bring progress to an end and to carry a purely static conception of "the good." This was, no doubt, not the meaning which Hobhouse intended or would have accepted, but his stress on harmony in personality seems to conflict with the conception of progress as dynamic and unending. Here, as elsewhere, sociology is peculiarly affected by the necessity of using language made for the looser general purposes of communication, not for logical or even descriptive exactitude.

I have dwelt upon the mind of Hobhouse, partly to illustrate my thesis that no worker in any of the human sciences can obtain an objectivity that is unaffected by his private physical and mental make-up and his personal history. But I have also wished to show how strongly my own intellectual life has been affected by long, close, direct personal intercourse with a student and thinker so much better equipped than myself in many lines of knowledge and capacities of thinking. For, entering the sphere of sociology through the portals of economic theory, I found my mind enlarged and enriched by a closer recognition of the various social studies that contribute to an understanding of the term "human welfare" which I had somewhat hastily imported into my presentment of economic value.

In other words, my growing repudiation of the efforts of economists to make of their study an exact quantitative science, with values expressed in purely monetary terms, was fortified by a clearer, fuller conception of the humanist interpretation to which I had been moving.

Another man whose writings and conversations had an influence on my thinking at this time was Graham Wallas. I first knew him at Oxford in the late seventies, but we did not come into close relations until I came to London in the late eighties. His Fabian Essay and his *Life of Francis Place** were early indications of his later important contribution to the art of politics. He ranks as the most original exponent of the psychology of modern politics both in its individual and social aspects, exhibiting more clearly than any other writer the interactions of rational and irrational elements in the play of political life. *Human Nature in Politics* and *The Great Society* exhibit an independence of mind and

* London: George Allen & Unwin, Ltd.

a practical knowledge of political thinking only attainable by one who has achieved his psychology by a long experience of administrative work. He and Hobhouse rank together in my experience as practical reformers, profoundly interested in the great happenings of their times, but always bringing their judgment on these happenings to a rational criterion of human value. Wallas broke away from the Fabian Society because it failed to denounce the Boer War and because of its early leaning toward Protection. Both he and Hobhouse remained pronounced Free-traders, and Hobhouse, when he left Manchester for London, acted for some time as secretary of the Free Trade Union. Both of them became teachers of politics and sociology in the newly formed London School of Economics, and were chief instruments in keeping alive the broad humanism of social teaching when there was a danger of over-cautious specialization in an institution whose earliest finance was derived from a convert to Socialism in the florid days of the Fabian Society when preaching meant business. If my fellow-townsman, Jonathan Hutchinson, had foreseen that his money would go into paying Professor Foxwell for teaching why not to socialize banking, Mr. Ackworth why not to nationalize the railways, I think he would have "turned in his grave." But Hobhouse and Wallas, though little concerned with practical socialism, remained firm exponents of human values in social movements and institutions, and stood for justice, equality, and humanity in all vital issues of their time. Though I was not associated with the School of Economics, save as a casual lecturer, my journalism and political-economic interests brought me into continual touch with one or both of these great men.

CHAPTER VII

POLITICS AND JOURNALISM

SETTLING down for the winter in Boston after my Canadian travels in 1905, I was recalled by an urgent request of Hobhouse to join him in the editorial work of the newly established *Tribune*. The venture was short-lived and unfortunate. My own connection was brief, for I soon discovered how ill fitted I was for a daily journalism that needed resources of information and presentation which I did not possess. After ceasing my daily attendance, I continued, however, to write special articles until the paper passed out of existence.

Then came a new and a far more interesting experience as a writer in the *Nation* under the brilliant editorship of H. W. Massingham. From 1906 to 1920 much of my political and other writing went into this weekly publication. While in its earlier years many of my articles were devoted to current politics, I had scope in the form of "middles" and reviews for other topics of a broader sociological character, many of them relating to my growing sense of the interdependence of politics, economics, and ethics.

But an even more valuable influence upon my views and sentiments was the free talk at the weekly lunches where for many years the regular contributors to the *Nation* met and to which distinguished outside visitors of this and other countries were invited. Its unique value lay in the frank utterances of men representing wide divergencies of mentality and political opinions, yet holding the common title of liberal. I have only to mention a few names in order to make good this statement. A company containing H. W. Massingham, L. T. Hobhouse, H. W. Nevinson, F. W. Hirst, C. F. G. Masterman, J. L. Hammond, the Rev. W. D. Morrison was bound to exhibit wide diversity of opinions upon many topics of current interest. Yet the skill of Massingham and of our friend Richard Cross, Chairman of the Directors, and a master in the art of conciliation, not merely kept our controversies within bounds, but gave to our writings a reasonable measure of consistency which made the *Nation* a real influence in the new trend of Liberalism.

I have sometimes felt regret that I was never able to pursue my economic studies in the quiet atmosphere of an academic life where I could have developed in a more orderly way my humanist theory, and tested it by lectures and discussions among serious-minded students. But I never had this opportunity. Though I spent most of my time in early middle life as a University Extension Lecturer, I was never invited to apply for any professorship in an English University. I had one or two invitations to posts in America, which I declined. Though I was in friendly contact with the founders of the London School of Economics, it was never suggested that I should go upon the staff. Though

I once allowed my name to be put forward for membership of the Political Economy Club, I heard no more of the proposal, and I have never written for the *Economic Journal*, though I have been for many years a member of the Society. My exclusion from organized academic economics has, therefore, been almost complete. I have already explained why this happened, and must have happened, as an inevitable consequence of an early heresy. Looking back, I do not now regret this exclusion from orthodox economic circles. For the mixed life of lecturing, controversial politics, and journalism into which I was driven, though in some ways damaging to orderly thinking, had compensations that were very valuable. Brought into touch with active leaders of political, economic, and ethical reform in various countries, I became increasingly aware of the common human element in these movements and of the distinctive part played by economic interests and urges. Nor was it only the experience of travel in various countries that enlarged my understanding of economic theory and processes, taking them out of the textbook mould and putting them in their proper human significance. During the most formative period of my thinking, I was fortunate in living near a little Surrey village sometimes described as "a nest of Socialists," because Sydney Olivier, Edward Pease, and one or two other Fabians lived near by, and other "revolutionaries" were frequent residents or visitors. Kropotkin was one of the most remarkable figures, and gave me interesting instruction in the theory and right practice of anarchism, while Bernstein preached the milder strain of Marxism. My anti-Imperialism was fed by visits from the South African statesmen Merriman and Sauer, while conversations with the greatest of Indian political thinkers, Gokhale, helped me to understand something of the amazing difficulties of our Imperial Government in its attempt to combine liberal development with forcible repression.

Here I would put in a plea for the free and fragmentary intercourse I have been describing as a mode for the discovery and communication of truth. In certain high intellectual quarters journalism has always been treated as the lowest form of printed matter, as vulgar necessity, no doubt, but degrading in its thought and literary form, with injurious reactions alike upon the mind of its writers and its readers. Now such disparagement is lacking in discrimination, and savours too much of intellectual arrogance. The hasty unchecked publication of news and opinions which strict "journalism" implies has obvious dangers to truth and literary style. Even weekly journalism (a contradiction in terms!) must in some degree be open to these charges. But in its best form, in the current commentary upon important events, it has virtues of its own to set against and qualify the defects of its hasty production. Not only has it a vitality and bite of thought, feeling, and expression, caught from the immediacy of the happenings it handles, but its very fragmentation evades some of the dangers that beset the longer, formal, more scientific, and philosophical expositions which claim the seats of intellectual authority. For thinking is in itself a brief fragmentary process, and the piecing together of these fragments into a system of thought, a science, or a philosophy, is seldom (never in the sphere of human conduct) the purely objective, disinterested, reasonable process it professes to be. A completely consistent history, or still more a philosophy, is invalidated, partly because it overrates the rationality of evolutionary thinking, partly because it is hampered by deficiencies of the instrument of language invented for purely practical purposes of communication.

If, however, we agree that nearly all thinking is done in brief spurts, mostly suggested or directed by some personal experience or current event, and is accompanied by some emotional activity which helps to determine its aims and values, we shall recognize a unique position for the best kind of journalism as current commentary. When we realize life in terms of values, we shall realize how the source of value and the processes of relation differs not only in different persons but in the same person with the changes and chances of life. The philosophic demand for absolute values, in truth, beauty, and goodness, lose much of their authority and meaning when confronted with the actual concrete experiences of life. It is no idle taunt to say that philosophy bakes no cakes, or is of no help to a philosopher with toothache. There is no doubt an intellectual satisfaction in pushing consistency and law into their highest reaches. But this does not justify the contempt for fragmentary thought and feeling and their expression in journalism. It is, however, right for me to limit this defence of journalism to writing done under fair and free conditions. The "middles" of the best weekly papers are here "the golden mean," giving the best expression to the fragmentary wisdom of the mind and pen. In the prose writings of our generation there have been many large literary and philosophic treatises of high intellectual merit. But their very height and length are limitations to the influence which they exert: for such prolonged expositions in high thinking evoke some suspicion of artificiality even among the minority of qualified readers. I think that there exists a widespread feeling, almost a belief, that wisdom comes in short runs. Perhaps the most striking instance in our literature is Bacon's *Essays*, the force and drive of which far exceed those of his more formal treatises. Coming nearer to journalism, one might cite the piecemeal utterances of Addison and Steele, of Johnson, Hazlitt, as examples of portable wit and wisdom which outlive most larger literary edifices. Within the last generation I find more vitality and fineness of expression in the journalistic work of Lowes Dickinson, H. W. Nevinson, Havelock Ellis, J. A. Spender, A. G. Gardiner, H. N.

Brailsford, and Ivor Brown than in all the more formal volumes of contemporary prose. It is not merely that these able, well-equipped writers have embarked, as editors and writers, upon a distinctively journalistic career—one or two of them have not—but because the article or essay furnishes a better vehicle for their variety and versatility of interests in the life in which they live and move and have their being, are in other words, a better expression for their humanism.

But, it may be said, do not your own pretensions as a reformer in economic theory transcend the fragmentation you here approve? If you do not lay claim to a complete system of humanist economics, you do pretend to put a logically defensible order on to the several heresies you have evoked. Psychology, with the secret defensive weapons rightly imputed to it, obliges me to hesitate here between a defence and an admission. The chief attraction of modern psychology, with its inhibitions and sublimations, lies in the humour of its revelations. It pleases us to discover underneath the parade of public spirit, disinterested regard for truth, justice, and the good of others, the secret play of some natural urge towards self-importance, acquisition, or other private satisfaction. But in its endeavour to spread its net over a wide field of inquiry, is there not some risk of neglecting the finest and most profitable fruits of humorous revelation, oneself. Psychology should make every man his own humorist, for the study of other psyches can only be derived from study of our own; the standards which every objective study requires can only be those which form our own inner experience. The finest, the most penetrating, humour lies in the discovery that the disinterested motives that have been figuring in the foreground of our own consciousness and have been feeding our sense of self-approval are to a large extent the servile tools of the primitive lusts for power and self-importance, or else protective weapons for the customary habits and institutions which give us status and security. But though the most ancient of psychologists bade us "Know thyself," few have been willing to follow that knowledge when it damages our customary self-esteem. Now intellectual self-esteem requires us to believe that our thinking is purely disinterested and that our public spirit and philanthropy are untainted by any self-seeking. The terminology of psychology in its elevated character promotes this self-deception, and is in part designed to do so. Pugnacity is "sublimated" on the football field, and is feigned to be subordinate to skill and dexterity, but the processes of kicking, scrum, and tackling are none the less fighting processes. Applied to man's work in science and philosophy, though the outside student of the mental processes may succeed in imputing pure logic to the reasoning involved, no faithful observer of his own scientific or philosophic thinking can fail to recognize the moulding influence of pre-existent interests and devices, hopes and fears, in the selection, direction, and evaluation of the mental movements. In economics and other social "sciences" this secret psychical play is more apparent than in other's thinking. I have already indicated how the *laisser-faire* economics of the nineteenth century and the Marxian economics which accompanied and followed were, with a crudity itself humorous, moulded by class interests and desires. I am now faced with the reasonable request "Physician, heal thyself." For it "stands to reason" that I cannot claim for myself an objectivity and disinterestedness which I have denied to others. Indeed, the biographic details in which I have indulged ought to help to explain not only the steps along which my economic thinking has proceeded, but the slipperiness of these very steps, and the likelihood, perhaps certainty, that my economic humanism, a composition of successive heresies, is defective when regarded as a whole. The psychology of heresy is a subject that has not received the attention it deserves. Orthodoxy, the acceptance of authoritative theories and opinions, apart from their intrinsic truth or value, is an attitude of mental and social security, a disposition to swim with the tide and to enjoy the benefits of respectability. Orthodoxy may be the right creed it claims to be, and its followers may give a reasonable acceptance to it. But it carries an inertia, an indisposition to question and criticize, and this pacific tendency is an enemy of progress. For progress can only come by a break away from authority or convention. But this break-away disposition is not necessarily the free play of a reasonable mind. It may be a pugnacious self-assertion of superiority over the accepted thought or faith of others. It is more attractive to fight for one's own property than for the common good. It is undeniable that a heresy becomes an intellectual property which rouses in its owner a sense of scarcity value and of personal attachment that are liable to lead him into methods of defence which carry stormy emotional bias and may cause him to transgress the bounds of sweet reasonableness. Thus it is difficult to determine at the outset whether a heresy is a genuinely rational product, the logical correction of wrong thinking, or whether it is a more or less plausible attempt to be peculiar, and to feel superior, in one's thinking. Even when one heresy is followed by others which appear to be its reasonable consequences, the sequence may be inspired by a subconscious personal urge towards a system which shall be our property and shall force its way into a newly won authority. How far I have succumbed to these temptations it is not possible for me to know. But as part of my interest as heretic has lain in watching the origins of my beliefs, and in enjoying the humour of the unexpected, as ideas come out of the sub-conscious, I may hope to have escaped some of that dogmatic overconfidence which is the besetting sin of heretics. At any rate, I can formally disclaim the pretence that I have woven my heresies into a complete economic system which will stand the test of future changes and the inroads of future heretics. Some order and causative connection I claim for my heresies, but not the unity, still less the permanence, of an economic system.

CHAPTER VIII

THE GREAT WAR AND ITS AFTERMATH

THIS at any rate was the situation up to the Great War when stronger divergencies of thought and feeling impaired the solidarity of membership in the groups with which I had contacts. The War was, indeed, a disrupting influence in every organization and movement with which I was associated. Most of these were by name or character democratic, pacifist, anti-Imperialist, and the War was an acid test for all such professions. Several of the active leaders in the pacifist movement, H. W. Perris (one of my closest friends for many years), J. R. Green, Victor Fisher, and Maddison, leaders in the peace movement, became strong supporters of a war policy, which would justify itself from their pacifist standpoint as "a war to end war." But this "peace" policy was an interesting psychological disclosure. Peace is in itself a negative conception, and perfect peace, like complete security, can have little positive emotional appeal. But when a minority group of pacifists is organized against war, it becomes a combative body, conducts "campaigns"; and its leaders are by natural selection "fighting men." This was the case with the men I have mentioned. Their natural pugnacity had helped them to leadership, and when the War came on it swept aside their pacifism and carried them forward into the wider field of conflict. But the Peace Movement in the years before the War suffered from another defect, in common with other aspects of the Democratic Movement. There was no real belief in the possibility of any early large-scale war, or in such a collapse ot democracy as followed. The long period of peace in Western Europe, the steady progress of popular self-government in all civilized countries, had fastened these achievements upon our minds as permanent testimonials to rationalism and ethics in the field of politics. This confidence in peaceful democracy as an accepted principle of political evolution became (as we now see) a source of weakness when a sudden challenge was presented. Pacifists were disconcerted by the discovery that the sort of peace in which they believed was unreal, just as later on democrats found themselves compelled for the first time to doubt the accepted methods of democracy.

In the pre-War period I, like others, found myself living in this atmosphere of illusion. It was not merely a popular illusion, it held the minds of the thoughtful minorities seriously concerned in politics.

Several members of the *Nation* group belonged also to a somewhat larger body known as the Rainbow Circle, which met monthly for free political and economic discussions. This title had no symbolic significance. Formed originally inside the National Liberal Club by Mr. Murray MacDonald, Mr. W. M.

Crook, and one or two other active radicals, it soon adjourned to the Rainbow Tavern in Fleet Street for its gatherings. After a year or two, owing, I believe, to shortcoming in its consumption of the more profitable forms of drink, it left this tavern and availed itself of the generous hospitality of Mr. (later Sir) Richard Stapley, who placed at its disposal a large room in his private residence, together with post-prandial amenities. Here for some twenty years I enjoyed the advantage of discussions carried on in an atmosphere of complete freedom, by politicians, journalists, civil servants, lawyers, clergymen, mostly men of conspicuous ability and extending from orthodox Liberals in the House of Commons to members of the Fabian Society and even the Social Democratic Federation. Among the most regular attendants were men of such diverse attachments as J. M. Robertson, Herbert Burrows, G. P. Gooch, Herbert Samuel, J. R. MacDonald, the Rev. A. L. Lilley, Russell Rea, Sydney Olivier, William Clarke, Percy Alden, Murray MacDonald, W. P. Reeves. Though several members of the Circle were Socialists, one or two revolutionists, the general atmosphere of complacency, to which I have alluded, enabled us to conduct our debates even on matters of high moment with good temper and reasonable argument.

Here again the War came as a disturbing revelation. Though no open breach in our good relations occurred, it became difficult for such anti-war men as Ramsay

MacDonald and Herbert Burrows to discuss matters of immediate moment with passionate ex-peace men like J. M. Robertson and W. P. Reeves. While the Circle was carried on for many years longer, it never quite recovered its early equanimity, and though fed by much younger blood did not develop the earlier sense of camaraderie. The belief in man as a rational and thoughtful being was shaken almost to destruction by the War, and all societies and organizations based upon this belief suffered accordingly.

It may come to be recognized that amid all the material and moral havoc which the War brought about, it performed one extremely salutary though disconcerting lesson, or perhaps two related lessons. Formerly we thought of civilized man as 80 per cent rational. We have now halved the percentage.

Again, it has, I think, been a misfortune that terms like rationalism and free-thought have been so tightly annexed by opponents of orthodox religion.* For

* It is true that the formal definition adopted by the Rationalist Press Association provides a wider field for Rationalism. "Rationalism may be defined as the mental attitude which unreservedly accepts the supremacy of reason and aims at establishing a system of philosophy and ethics verifiable by experience and independent of all arbitrary assumptions of authority." But there has been no attempt to establish any code of social or political ethics or to assert independence of authority in the economic field. The contents of the *Literary Guide* (the organ of the Rationalist Press) contain articles upon philosophical and literary topics but avoid any serious attention to Socialism, Communism, or Democracy in its economic bearing.

it is evident that the same medley of traditional emotionalism and magical beliefs which composes the sentiment of religious orthodoxy is present in the creeds and sentiments of political and economic orthodoxy. In politics Monarchy remains a divine institution, endowed, as the recent ceremony of the Coronation testifies, with a sanctity and mysticism designed to remove it from rational assessment. Divine right and supernatural authority, though no longer openly claimed, still lurk in the ceremonial of the anointment and the sacramental rite. But this spirit of sanctity is by no means confined to Monarchy. The glorification of the nation and the empire, as illustrated in school ceremonial and teaching, and in political meetings, does not differ, save in degree, from the cruder practices of Nazism and Fascism. The sacred emotionalism, poured out before the image of an empire bound in close solidarity by a common language, common interests and sympathies, can only be produced by keeping out of view the racial, linguistic, and other conflicts of interest visible in each of our dominions, in most of our colonies, and especially in the country that gives us our chief claim to magnitude of area and population, India.

Turning from politics to economics and the class distinctions connected with grades of income, can it be questioned that property and the legal ways of acquisition are kept from close rational scrutiny by a traditional and well-cultivated regard for "rights"?

Any political changes which can be presented as an invasion of the "rights" of property have a flavour of wickedness about them. Any abolition of class distinctions connected with reputable modes of earning incomes carries at least a presumption of wrong-doing. The differences of manner, bearing, speech, between the gentry and the common people, are still accepted and valued as genuine contributions to the varied interests of national life. These differences have declined in intensity of feeling from eighteenth-century ruralism to modern urbanity, but they remain strongly marked even in the blending of large city life. Though the sentiment of "worship" only remains for royalty, various grades of "reverence" still attach to the upper classes; gentility and respectability are qualities retaining some emotional value.

This refusal to apply clear reasoning to unveil the defects of political and economic institutions, and the social respectabilities and class distinctions associated with them, is in some measure due to the stubborn objection of "rationalists" to apply to property, income, profit, and other economic concepts the same relentless logic they apply to religious concepts. Few of them have gone so far as to explore the measure of truth which underlies Marx's assertion that religion is the dope of capitalism.

While, then, the ethical movement is founded upon the conviction that morality is independent of theology, goodness having a directly human origin and appeal, the willingness to apply moral tests to social institutions, especially to economic practices, has not been a generally accepted usage. The tendency has been to use ethics as an emotional substitute for religion rather than as a general guide to social and personal conduct. There is, however, in recent times a disposition among the younger members of ethical societies, and to a less extent among "rationalists," to bring their ethics and their rationalism to bear upon problems of social progress. Social-economic equality is becoming an accepted end for ethical agitation,* and though the publications of the rationalist Press show little disposition to apply to social problems the fuller rationalism of Thomas Paine, Godwin, and Robert Owen, an increasing number of its leaders devote their main energy to the propagation of reforms in economic, political, and educational fields. Rationalism and free-thinking are thus gradually broadening out into instruments for bringing clear consciousness into processes of social evolution. Practical experience of the difficulties attending this process made me aware of the strength of conservatism in resisting the new demands for social justice and a reasonable economic order. For if the course of events has been such as I describe among those who profess reason and justice for their guides, what can be expected from those who

* The Society to Promote Human Equality is a recent vigorous outcome of the ethical movement, receiving its chief support from Mr. R. Arnold Price and other active Ethicists.

regard the traditional ways of acquiring and using property, and the economic system engaged in these processes, as part of the order of nature and outside the bounds of rational inquiry? But while most members of the possessing and ruling classes thus accept their property and power as needing no defence, the more intelligent minority, who fear encroachments from the workers as trade unionists and citizens inflamed by Socialist propaganda, are grateful for the reasoned protection provided by academic and Press "defenders of the faith."

CHAPTER IX

POLITICAL AND ECONOMIC CONSEQUENCES OF THE WAR

THOUGH in the pre-War epoch there was widespread discontent with the failure of real wages to rise as they had risen in the preceding periods, the discontent had no revolutionary character. The spirit and traditions of our people had never imbibed the sort of revolutionary spirit prevalent in some continental peoples; partly, because we believed ourselves to possess popular self-government applicable to the bettering of our conditions; partly, because of an element of caution in our character which prevented our resort to quick, simple, and violent remedies. Though, as will be seen, post-War disturbances have had some effect on our traditional attitudes, the failure of our workers, even of a professedly Socialist Labour Party, to agree upon any general intelligible policy attests the truth of my assertion that the application of reason and justice to drastic reforms is or appears to lie outside the limits of our national character. It may be that the conservatism of the cliché, "human nature being what it is," can be overcome by some power of "sudden conversion" in the political-economic mentality. But until and unless that happens it seems foolish either to desire or to fear any "revolutionary" policy in this country.

My pre-War experience, as teacher, journalist, traveller, and general mixer in movements and groups, went to confirm my earlier view that progress would come by a concessionaire policy of the owning classes, together with elements of economic betterment for the workers achieved by public policy and finance. This, at any rate, seemed to be the path to be taken by a people averse alike to idealistic theories and revolutionary practices and conscious of their power to bend their popular Government to meet their urgent economic needs. The temporary stoppage of rising wages during the pre-War period was compensated by old-age pensions, better provision for the poor, and improvements in education, health, and other social services. Though a Labour Party, formally addicted to Socialism, showed signs of growth in all industrial centres and in Parliament, it was not seriously regarded as a menace to the rule of the possessing classes and their Government.

The War struck several blows at this complacency. In the first place, it showed that in British democracy the people and their elected representatives had no effective control over foreign policy with its vital issues of peace and war. Secondly, it showed that while several millions of able-bodied workers were taken from the productive into the destructive services, and the wealth of the nation was lavished recklessly upon the expenses of the War, huge profits were acquired by the owners and managers of the businesses directly or indirectly engaged on armaments, ships, and other favoured industries, while the civilian workers had a higher standard of living than before. Thirdly, it soon became evident that this was no "war to end war," but an exhibition of unfettered national sovereignty, and that the only way of ending war was through constructive internationalism.

Though the popular enthusiasm for the War and the efforts to fight and work which it involved, together with the voluntary submission to all restrictions and impositions laid down by the War Government, prevented these truths from gaining full recognition, thinking minorities began without delay to organize so as to deal with the menaces to democracy, liberty, and peace.

But before turning to these endeavours to stem the tide of war, it is worth while recording the brief effort to keep this country out made in the days preceding August 1914, by a small Neutrality Group. When war seemed imminent, this group, containing Lord Courtney, Lowes Dickinson, Graham Wallas, Gilbert Murray, and a few others, sought through the Press to get a hearing for neutrality. My only personal contribution to this cause was the annexation of Lord Bryce, just returned from America, whom I tracked on Saturday afternoon to a place in Camden Town where he was personally engaged in unpacking trunks of books. His name would undoubtedly have carried more weight than all the rest of us, if circumstances had not made the attempt too late. Sir Edward Grey's speech in the House of Commons on Monday made our entry to the War inevitable, and our little Committee dissolved. This was the first of a series of shocks to my belief that the world was inhabited by a reasonable animal.

The most active of anti-war agencies during the War and for some years after was the Union of Democratic Control (for Foreign Policy). Formed in the early autumn of 1914 by a little group of politicians, among whom E. D. Morel, Ramsay MacDonald, A. Ponsonby, C. Trevelyan, Norman Angell were leaders, it soon drew into its ranks scattered groups throughout the country who held that we were dragged into a war by Grey and a secret junta of the Cabinet, and that it was of urgent importance to get as soon as possible a negotiated peace, and to provide Parliament with direct knowledge of and control over all treaties and other engagements which entailed future risks of war. Sitting on the Executive Committee of this Society almost from its beginning, I came to learn a good deal of the doubts and difficulties carried in the term "Democratic Control." Should a Committee of the House of Commons, representative of all parties, exercise this control? This sounded democratic. But in a party government it would sin against the first principle of governmental responsibility. The Government for internal affairs must also be the Government for external affairs. Important international issues, such as tariffs and commercial treaties, cannot be removed from Government control. But, it was urged, the Commons Committee need not have determinate control; it need only be a source of information for the House and the country. But here, too, there were objections on the ground that necessary diplomacy would be damaged if each step were made public to the House of Commons. Some secrecy was necessary though it should not be carried so far as our engagements with France before the War. Strong views upon this subject, pro and con, held by several of our members, prevented the development and application of the very principle that was our *raison d'être*. This did not, however, sterilize our activities, it simply drove them into agitation against conscription and in favour of measures for an early peace. But more might have been accomplished, had it not been for the distrust and antipathy which soon appeared between Morel and Ramsay MacDonald. Morel's audacious flaming oratory and a certain recklessness of consequences repelled the cautious and calculating nature of MacDonald. An atmosphere of conflict thus impaired the unity of the Committee. One of our members rudely described the situation in the language of Oliver Wendell Holmes as that of "two prize bulls in one three-acre lot." For at that time MacDonald had a dominating personality, and showed a certain jealousy of the masterfulness to which Morel also inclined. There were no open ructions, but after the

War was over, and Morel began to make great progress as a Labour politician in the country, winning a Parliamentary seat, the divergence of the two leaders became so evident that, when Morel was left out of the appointments in MacDonald's first Government, no surprise was felt by those who understood their relations. Morel as Foreign Minister, with fuller knowledge of foreign affairs than any other Labour man, might have made history by easing the peace terms and bettering our relations with Germany. But equally he might have failed through trying to carry us further and faster than we could be persuaded to go. Such speculations are not profitable. I mention them because this incident helped to bring home to me the immense part played by personal factors in those vital issues which demand disinterested consideration for their settlement.

The project of a League of Nations for the preservation of world peace took shape during the first year of the War in the discussions of a small group summoned by G. Lowes Dickinson and Richard Cross under the Chairmanship of Lord Bryce. The idea, of course, was by no means a war-product. It had a distinguished ancestry among European thinkers during several centuries, and a few years before the War was developed by Sir G. Paish and placed before statesmen in America. During the War the idea of a League of Nations to maintain world peace was in the minds of Englishmen like Sir Edward Grey and Americans like

Taft, Colonel House, and Wilson. A League of Nations Society was set up on a small scale in 1915 by Lord Parmoor, Lord Courtney, and a few others, afterwards to be merged with the League of Free Nations Association founded early in 1918, so as to form "The League of Nations Union" with Grey as its first President. But the Bryce scheme, published in the spring of 1915,* as a result of a long series of discussions, was the first formal draft of the League as brought into political life by the efforts of President Wilson and General Smuts. Service on this Bryce Committee, with my friends Graham Wallas, Hobhouse, and Lowes Dickinson, was my first initiation into the mysteries and delicacies of internationalism as a practical policy.

Though it is not possible here to set forth the full proposals in the Bryce Report, its character is faithfully indicated in the following passage from the "Introduction":

> "The members, then, of our proposed Union would bind themselves by treaty
>
> (1) To refer all disputes that might arise between them, if diplomatic methods of adjustment had failed, either to an arbitral tribunal for judicial decision, or to a council of conciliation and report.
>
> (2) Not to declare war or begin hostilities or hostile

* London: George Allen & Unwin, Ltd.

preparations until the tribunal has decided, or the council has reported.

(3) To take concerted action, economic and forcible, against any signatory Power that should act in violation of the preceding condition.

(4) To take similar action against any non-signatory Power that should declare war or begin hostilities or hostile preparations against a signatory Power, without first submitting the dispute to peaceable settlement by the method indicated in (1)."

It will be noted that this draft does not propose to apply a sanction to the awards of the Court but only to the refusal of Powers to submit their case to the Court for consideration and award.

The League of Nations Society, formed later on during the War, went further than the Bryce proposals in its application of Sanctions to the awards of the Court, and the American League to Enforce Peace also supported the same policy, though confining it to action against an aggressive member of the League.

The chief interest in the Bryce report is that it rightly measured the assent that could at that time be secured for the idea of international action. To a few of its signatories the inadequacy of this internationalism for the purpose of world security seemed evident. My own view was that our scheme did not take adequate account of the economic inequality of nations, in regard to the resources of the country or of colonies under their control, as a source of discord and strife. This view I set forth at some length in my book *Towards International Government*,* published in the summer of 1915. The pressure exercised by important industrial, commercial, and financial interests in "capitalist" countries upon their Governments to obtain foreign markets for their surplus products and foreign areas of development for their surplus capital, has played a predominant part in that process of imperialism which is an increasing source of conflict between the "haves" and the "have not" nations. Though countries like Germany, entering late upon the capitalist system, long viewed with jealous eyes the huge empire, a quarter of the habitable globe, held by Britain under the titles of Empire, Dominions, Colonies, Protectorates, and spheres of influence, this envy was kept within pacific bounds so long as free and equal access to its markets was maintained. But as soon as the Dominions set restrictions on their markets and upon immigration, while the War converted the whole Empire into a preferential preserve, beginning the cancelment of our Free Trade policy, the division between the "haves" and the "have nots" came into clear consciousness as a lasting cause of discord.

No International Council, such as was proposed,

* London: George Allen & Unwin, Ltd.

could ignore what seemed to be the chief modern cause of war. For though other more reputable causes —security, pride, prestige—figured in the foreground and inflamed war-passions, the real conflict of vital interests between nations lay in the economic field. This is frequently denied by those who cite the Great War as a non-economic event. But while it is true that the possessive passion has other appeals, it is idle to contend that Alsace-Lorraine, with her natural resources, the *Drang nach Osten*, the scramble for North Africa, Persia, China, Constantinople, and the access to the Mediterranean, were not economic in their main significance. Such are the really "vital" interests which divide nations, easy and growing access to foods and raw materials, increasing and reliable markets for surplus home products, areas for migration of growing population under their own flag, or free access to foreign areas of profitable development. These economic considerations seemed to me of paramount importance in any project aiming at an international order. Fair play for the several advanced nations with their expanding trade and population, security for the interests of the backward peoples in areas thus opened to development and migration, and more broadly the utilization of the world's economic resources for the equal benefit of all mankind—such was the practical ideal which a League of Nations or other international system should envisage and seek to attain.

It was evident to us that such a path involved the existence of an International Government, implying the surrender of important elements of sovereignty by individual States. It has taken eighteen years' experience of the League of Nations to bring a recognition of this necessity, and the lesson is not yet learnt. But the demand made by Germany for colonies or other enlargements of territory, in order to meet her vital needs for markets and for occupation, is bringing the League to realize that without powers to deal with such demands upon the part of its actual or potential members, it cannot secure the peace of the world. Hence the movement towards economic congresses and schemes for equal distribution of raw materials. But those conferences and schemes will come to nothing so long as they rely upon the willingness of the "have" nations to make concessions to the "have nots." The request by Germany for a return of her confiscated colonies makes it evident that such altruism will not work. So long as internationalism has no super-sovereignty over nationalism and no power to enforce the international will, the equality of economic opportunity needed for a secure peace is unattainable. The belief entertained by a few *laisser-faire* politicians and economists that equal access to economic utilities can be attained without any cessions of political ownership or control is not valid. Economic equality demands either a definite cession of colonial possessions by the "haves" to the "have nots," irrespective of the consent of the inhabitants, or a pooling of all such possessions under an international government. It was not possible in 1919 to endow a League with such sovereign powers. It may still be impracticable, with only three of the seven Great Powers as reliable members. But it would be well to recognize that dependence either upon mutual goodwill or community of interests, is inadequate to get down the barriers to free economic intercourse and to meet the demands for equal access to raw materials and equal rights of migration.

It is becoming more and more evident, also, that a dominant underlying issue is that of population. For though pride of possession may count heavily, the possessive motive rests ultimately upon the vital need of finding food and the land on which to grow it for increasing national populations. If an international government with powers to regulate the supplies of foods and raw materials through free commercial intercourse could also regulate the growth of populations in the different countries, all the chief sources of conflict between nations might disappear. Since this is at present unattainable, a League competent to secure world peace must at any rate be endowed with the right to regulate the rate and direction of the migration of populations so as to promote the best development of world resources with the least disturbance of national life.

Such a League, with the requisite sovereign

powers ceded by the member nations, was clearly contemplated by many sanguine promoters of the League, who recognized that without such powers permanent peace could not be secured. The history of the post-War world has, however, shown that none of the Great Powers is yet ready for this necessary surrender of its sovereign rights. It is this perverted nationalism which is now seen to block the path of progress and to threaten the very existence of civilized life. It is this nationalism which prevents politicians and peoples from realizing the vicious nature of the barriers which block trade and impede intercourse between nations. But until the domination of class and economic interests within each nation, which feeds and inspires this nationalism, can be recognized and overcome by an enlightened classless nationalism, a League of Nations will not be endowed with the authority and the power needed for world peace and progress.

The great lesson of the War and the even more important lesson of the Peace thus brought home to me the truth that justice as well as charity begins at home. It is impracticable to hope for peace and justice in international affairs unless the conditions for internal peace and justice within the nations have already been substantially obtained. It was this thought that linked up my special economic studies of over-saving and under-consumption with my wider political and economic outlook. I thus got a glimpse of the ideology of the new situation in which democracy, as hitherto conceived, was destined to be torn between capitalism and proletarianism, each seeking to use the machinery of the State for economic mastery, and driven by the emergency of the conflict to dictatorships of the right or left.

But for some time the atmosphere was very hazy. The prevalent feeling when the War came to an end was that after a time things would settle down in their old grooves, and that after some licking of wounds, the different combatant nations would somewhat shyly resume their earlier relations. Though some foresaw that grave troubles would come from reparations, War debts, and new frontiers, few, if any, had any notion of the disastrous psychological reactions of the post-War blockade and the Versailles Treaty upon the German people.

Most of my associates in the world of politics and journalism lived in an atmosphere of hope. The War had broken many bonds of custom, had evoked a wide sense of comradeship, and made large advances in social reforms possible and politically necessary. "Self-determination" had a captivating sound and the liberation of Poland and other oppressed nationalities seemed an earnest of a new Liberal Europe. Above all, the Russian Revolution appeared to give a fine refutation to the dull doctrine of gradualness. Smuts's famous statement, "The tents have been struck and the great Caravan of humanity is once more on the march,'' was a true expression of this challenge of hope. But the ''whither'' of the march remained obscure. This hope and obscurity were well illustrated for me on a small scale by the formation of the ''1917 Club.'' It was the Kerensky revolution of the spring, not the Lenin revolution of October, that initiated the Club, though it did not come into operation until the Communist regime was established. It had no declared aim or object but was a free meeting-place for ''advanced'' men and women concerned with political and economic reforms, or with new literary or artistic movements. Among the early adherents and contributors to its gatherings were Olive Schreiner, Ramsay MacDonald, Oswald Mosley, Bertrand Russell, H. W. Nevinson, E. M. Forster. Though no political creed was imposed or adopted, most of the members were formally or informally attached to the rising Labour Party, and, as time went on, a strong Communist flavour came to be recognized, especially among the younger members. On the whole, it was regarded as a club of ''intellectuals,'' and as such reflected the confusion of principles and policies that belonged to any attempt to ''understand'' and synthesize what was going on in war-sodden Europe.

Having no solid bond of creed or policy but only an ''atmosphere,'' it outlived its early fervour of spirit and passed into a convenient meeting-place until the financial embarrassments of high rents and low members' fees, often unpaid, brought it to a close.

Looking back on the pre-War and the War period I recognize that my politics and economics have been influenced by several other weighty personal associations. One of these was John Morley, with whom I was on friendly terms for twenty years, and of whom I saw a good deal during the War period. In many vivid post-lunch conversations he disclosed not only his horror at recent happenings but the nature of Victorian radicalism with its pacific *laisser-faire* humanitarianism in home and foreign politics. "Yesterday," he said to me in war-time, "I had a letter from an old friend in which he said, 'Morley, you once spelt God with a small g. You were right.' " But most of his brilliant talk related to the political past, and helped me much to understand how definitely sundered were economics and politics to the mind of Victorian statesmen. John Bright, able business man, politician, religious moralist of the strictest pattern, was, nevertheless, able to feel it his duty to resist legal attempts to limit factory hours and to safeguard the health of the workers in his mills. Yet Morley once told me that he would rather have been Bright than any other mid-Victorian statesman. Here he probably had in mind, not so much Bright's opinions as his wonderful power of oratory, a quality to which Morley could never aspire.

Another statesman with whom I had a long friendship and close contact during the War period was J. C. Smuts. Carrying personal introductions to him from two relations who knew him at Cambridge, I saw much of him in my South African visit in 1899, spending much of my time at Pretoria as a visitor in his home. As a statesman he was then "in the making": his task as State Attorney in conducting the delicate negotiations for Kruger's government with England was no light one, but he kept up a cheery countenance and a conversation in which commentaries on the Greek drama and the nursing of an infant "Chamberlain killer," reduced current controversies to a minimum. I did not then perceive how multifarious his abilities were destined to prove, as soldier, statesman, and philosopher. Even when nearly twenty years later I came again into close contact with him as adviser and member of our War Government, I did not realize the strength of the philosophic bent which was to find expression in his work on Holism. But it helped me to realize the impulse which has led several of the ablest statesmen of our time, Balfour, Haldane, Samuel, and Smuts to have recourse to the heights of philosophy as a refuge from the grave new issues pressing into the field of politics.

* * * *

Personal contacts with many men and women of advanced political views from "good Liberals" to Socialists and Communists during the immediate post-War period, gradually led me to understand what the War had done to "politics" by exposing its superficial operations and bringing it down to "brass tacks." Though, as we have seen, the social-economic problems which were sedulously kept in the background throughout the mid-Victorian epoch were beginning to show their heads in the nineties, and to infect party politics with inconvenient extensions of social services, the full significance of a politics in which organized labour sought to use the State for the control of economic life, productive, distributive, consumptive, was made manifest for the first time in the post-War period. Even then its full pressure did not occur until the time of the great depression. For though the decade following the Peace saw mighty changes in the political structure of most European countries, involving the financial and economic ruin of whole classes of the community and setting up new barriers to commercial intercourse, it was not until the world depression that the workers' demand to control Government and the capitalist resistance of that demand began to divide Europe into "reds" and "whites," "Fascists" and "Socialists." This division is very indistinct in England, and even in France, where logic has a fuller sway, there are several modifications of the cleavage. Indeed, everywhere, even in dictatorial countries, there is some pretence of shunning a sheer class cleavage under the cover of national unity.

But it remains true that the Great War and still more the Bad Peace have ripened and speeded up those class economic conflicts which were kept under by party policies of opportunist concessions before 1914. The pretence that capitalism is consistent with a real democracy in which the organized working classes can take their due part in Government, that "gradualness" along the old familiar lines can still suffice, wears thinner and thinner, as the recent course of events discloses.

To present the appearance of democracy, without handing over the reality of government to the people, had long been the unchallenged achievement of the upper classes in Britain and America. The machinery of two-party politics was successfully devoted to this end. How successfully I have shown in Victorian England, but in America the party machinery was even more cleverly applied, being less hampered by traditional allegiances and assisted by the limits of the federal system.

CHAPTER X

BREAK-UP OF CREEDS AND PARTIES

EVEN after the War, it seemed as if in this and other democratic countries, something like a restoration of pre-War conditions was feasible. The material havoc of the Great War was quickly repaired, many of the worst conditions of the Bad Peace were in process of correction: the monetary instability which impeded trade was in course of cure. Then came the Slump, worse, longer, and more general, than any previous one, and breaking upon peoples whose minds were no longer attuned to waiting for a natural recovery—after years of misery, poverty, and unemployment.

I am first concerned with the effect of this disaster upon the structure of political government, as I saw it in this country. The Liberal Party had already crumbled before the rise of a nominally Socialist Labour Party, placed in office, though hardly in power, by a popular vote largely drawn from former Liberals. The payment of Members helped to bring into keen politics the trade unions whose leaders saw their way to an honourable career in the House of Commons. The rank and file of the Labour Party are not Marxian or any other brand of Socialist, though they accept the title and send representatives to Conferences and Congresses which pass Socialist resolutions. Some of their leaders are Socialists in a secondary distant sense, their prime and immediate policy being the betterment of conditions in their own trade, with assistance from the State. A scattered minority in most cities and industrial areas have been getting education in Socialist principles from the handful of middle- and upper-class "intellectuals" whose thought and sympathies have led them to a fuller adoption of Socialism or Communism. But the wide gap in education and in personal bearing between the "workers" and the intellectuals makes solidarity of thought and policy a difficult process. Those who criticize the ineffectiveness of the Labour Party in Parliament, whether as Government or Opposition, should take account of these "class" distinctions with the misunderstandings and suspicions they involve. The basic cause of the collapse of the second Labour Government was the failure of most of its leaders and followers to realize the dangers of a financial situation which lay outside their understanding of politics and economics. The Nationalist Government which followed may be regarded as a testimony to the collapse of the older party distinctions rather than to the triumph of Conservatism which it seemed to many. For the fact is that the same opportunist Socialism which was the professed policy of the new Labour Movement permeated in milder degree the two older parties. Conservatism had throughout the nineteenth century been less closely attached to Capitalism than had

Liberalism. As Sir John Marriott has pointed out, most of the State interferences with private enterprise and *laisser-faire*, i.e. with capitalist dominion, were carried out by Conservative Governments in the teeth of Liberal opposition. Though in later times most industrial magnates have left a decaying Liberalism for the more potent and reputable Conservatism which they have helped to transform into a safeguard for Capital versus Labour, the Conservative Party still retains some of its traditional humanitarianism in the conduct of industry. The large increase of public expenditure on social services since the beginning of the nineties met much approval and but little opposition from Conservative statesmen, while their far-reaching influences have brought immense gains to the social and economic well-being of the working classes.*

Though the direct contributions of the employees to many of these services, together with the indirect

* The Report of P.E.P. (1937) (Political and Economic Planning) upon the Social Services groups them as follows:

(1) Constructive community services, including education, public health, and medical services, the mental health services, the welfare of the blind, and the work of the Ministry of Labour's employment exchanges and training centres.

(2) The social insurance services, including national health insurance, unemployment insurance, and widows', orphans' and old-age contributory pensions—the workmen's accident compensation scheme is also put in this class.

(3) The social assistance services, including non-contributory old-age pensions, the work of the Unemployment Assistance Board, and the manifold services of local public assistance committees.

taxation involved in a Protectionist policy of tariffs, embargoes, and subsidies, is a large qualification of this humanitarian policy, it none the less remains true that Conservatism is not a conscious technique of the defence of capitalism by a policy of minor concessions, but carries a new and more conscious interest in the welfare of the workers. There is, indeed, a little group of Conservatives whose "Socialism" carries them further in the reform policy than most Liberal politicians are yet prepared to go. While, therefore, the belief of most Conservatives in the "rights of property" and the control of industry by the owning class remains unimpaired and forms the basis of opposition to Socialism and Communism, this belief is modified or even undermined in the minds of an influential minority.

It is, however, in the Liberal Party that the shattering effects of recent events are most discernible. Free Trade, its most cherished policy, was a War casualty. For though the tariffs of the War Government were intended as emergency measures, their extension into the post-War period indicated the early jettisoning of the whole Free Trade system. During the War Liberals reluctantly bowed before the emergency and later on lent their support to its continuance for a period of post-War settlement. Then came the demand of the Dominions for a practical response to their voluntary preferences, and Liberals as a party were divided. Most leaders and the rank and file remained Free Traders "in principle," but it soon became evident that they could not look forward to an early escape from the now strongly rooted Protectionism, and when the Nationalist Government absorbed Sir John Simon and other old-school Liberals, it became clear that Free Trade, together with "economy" and anti-bureaucracy, the bulwarks of nineteenth-century Liberalism, were doomed to disappear. There remains a remnant of stalwarts who have refused to bow down in the House of Simon, and continue to hope for a revival of Liberalism on the ancient formula of Peace, Retrenchment, and Reform, though it is difficult to know what meaning they would attach to the last of the three terms. My old and valued friend, F. W. Hirst, is a revivalist of this order, convinced that with truth upon his side he will appeal successfully to the reasonable self-interest of the ordinary citizen for an escape from the entanglements of Protectionism, Militarism, and Imperialism.

A considerably larger section of this dwindling party takes what may be termed the middle course, developing, as in their "Five Years' Plan," a progressive Liberalism which does its best to advocate public control of key industries and finance, with extension of public services, on lines that elude the charge of Socialism by confining public ownership to a few national and municipal monopolies and leaving detailed administration of "controlled" industries in private hands. It seems possible that, if our electoral system were worked along the lines of Proportional Representation, a powerful Liberal Party could be created on this platform. For the rank and file of Labour is not enamoured of bureaucratic rule, and, if there were a reasonable likelihood of coalition with a powerful Liberal Party along the lines of the "Five Years' Plan," many electors who now vote Labour, without a close Labour attachment, would vote Liberal.

For this progressive Liberal policy is nearer to the average electoral mind than any full-blown Socialism. The strong distrust of officials (dubbed "bureaucrats") may seem excessive in view of the high general ability, honesty, and public spirit in our services. I think it is excessive, so far as the socialization of monopolies and routine industries is concerned. For in these industries the incentive of free competition is either absent or is wasteful in its operations. The danger that besets Labour-Socialism is its failure to recognize the fact that over a large area of industry, prize-money, in the shape of profit, must continue to be a serviceable method of getting the best results of inventive ability, risk, and enterprise, into the productivity of industry. The notion that a sense of public service will operate upon all types of mind so as to get the best they have to give in contributions towards technological and business ability, cannot be accepted for purposes of present practical progress.

The distinction here indicated between industries that can and should be "socialized" in ownership and control and those which cannot and should not, is one of the most important economic lessons to be learnt in our time. More and more, as I shall show, it has affected my own economic thinking, and my political attachments. For loosely but sincerely attached to Liberalism before the rise of a Labour Party, I formally resigned my membership when during the War Liberals of the Government abandoned Free Trade. The only time I stood for Parliament was in the 1918 election when I conducted a hopeless campaign as an Independent. Though since then my sympathies have been with the Labour Party, I have never felt quite at home in a body governed by trade union members and their finance, and intellectually led by full-blooded Socialists. For neither section of this Labour Party avowedly accepts that middle course which seems to me essential to a progressive and constructive economic government in this country. It may be that Socialism under its present leadership is shedding the dogmatism of its early shape. But it still seems a long way from the formulation of a policy which commands the intellectual assent and the moral enthusiasm needed to break the indifference and traditional servitude of the mass of an electorate unaccustomed to thinking and subject to the wily propaganda of "vested interests" in moments of real or fabricated crisis.

CHAPTER XI

POST-WAR ECONOMICS

So much for the war-havoc in party politics. Let me now turn to a topic more germane to the general purpose of this book, viz. the influence of the War and post-War events in this and other countries upon the "science" of economics. (May I note in passing the significant avoidance of the older term "Political Economy" at a time when political forces and actions influence economic thought and policy more than ever before?)

We saw that before the War "Economics" in this and other countries was moving in two opposite directions, towards a purely and exactly quantitative study of measured facts and tendencies, on the one hand, towards a "humanist" interpretation of these facts and tendencies, upon the other. This divergence had been greatly enlarged and accelerated by the War and its *sequelae*. The former tendency has been fed from two widely different sources. The prominence given to monetary changes and their visible reactions upon industry and commerce has pushed "the measuring rod" into the forefront of economic thought, and monetary-minded economists have been greatly encouraged in their insistence that supply and demand, and the "costs" and "utilities" which these terms serve, can only be usefully studied as statistical facts and forces. The natural predilection for exactitude which, as has already been pointed out, is part of the mental equipment of scientific students, has thus been strengthened by the instability of money, credit, prices, and exchange in the post-War world.

Mr. R. G. Hawtrey is the most authoritative exponent of purely monetary explanations of our economic troubles.

> "The real answer to all the non-monetary explanations of the depression is that they are merely particular cases of the monetary explanation. If they do not explain the shrinkage of demand, they do not explain the depression. And the shrinkage of demand is simply a shrinkage of the flow of money."*

It is, of course, true that in every depression there is a "shrinkage of demand" and "a shrinkage of the flow of money." This last Mr. Hawtrey attributes to something he calls "the inherent instability of credit" without explaining why this instability is "inherent." For why does the flow of money, i.e. credit, shrink at certain places in the trade cycle? Apart from "shrinkage of demand" in general, there may occur misapplications of demand. If, as I contend, such misapplication occurs in normal periods of

* *Trade Depression*, p. 100.

production by an excessive demand for capital-goods and a defective demand for consumption-goods, would this be rightly termed "a monetary explanation"? If credit shrinks because of a discovered excess in the demand for plant and other capital goods, owing to maldistribution of income, this cannot be regarded as a monetary explanation. The second source of this mathematical trend is, I frankly admit, more disputable. It is related to a half-conscious desire, both among academic and business "economists," to defend the current capitalist system against the new serious assaults to which it is exposed by Socialism, Communism, and Trade Unionism seeking to use political power and ethical appeals for the furtherance of "revolutionary" aims. This can best be done, this order of economist believes, by an intellectual insistence upon the isolation of economics from other "social" activities and interests, and its presentation in "laws," "principles," and "tendencies" that are purely objective and quantitatively presentable. This is partly a survival, partly an extension of the *laisser-faire* competitive individualism of the Ricardian economics. Its leading exponents are genuinely afraid of the incursion of "humanism" into their science, from sentimental and idealistic sources. They realize how woefully defective the reasoning of Marxist and other full-fledged Socialists can be, how selfishly narrow many of the trade union tactics are, and they recognize themselves as "defenders of the faith."

What they fail to recognize is that they are turning themselves into the mercenary or volunteer protectors of a capitalism which has outlived the period of its utility, and of a profiteering system no longer serviceable even in the interests of maximum productivity. This blindness has subtle psychological implications. In America, Veblen and others have pointed out with irrefutable arguments the part played in the economics of the colleges by the selection of "safe" teachers and methods of study, warranted not to offend the well-to-do benefactors and trustees. In England this aspect of the issue has not the same prominence. The defence of capitalism, the repudiation of dangerous doctrines, is not a direct conscious motive in the mind of our economists. It proceeds, partly from a genuine belief in the rightness of the established system and of the "economics" which expand and justify intellectually this system, partly from a sincere rejection of the Socialist case, as expounded by its literature. But it is none the less closely associated with a strong class feeling for friends and associates whose interests lie in the preservation of the capitalist system. It is not possible to escape the power of early associations and the social standards of education, manners, and ways of living of those with whom we have been thrown. Equality of educational opportunities has not yet gone nearly far enough to break these bonds, and they continue to restrict the minds of those who are called upon to formulate and expound the political, social, and, above all, the economic principles of the world around them. Though it is not possible to give any exact account of an academic atmosphere, purposely kept vague, it is certain that its canons of respectability and its sympathy with the culture of the upper classes predispose it to the intellectual support of the current social-economic system. While this disposition does not imply any lack of philanthropy, it has been distinctly favourable to an economics that prides itself on detachment from sentimental values.

But the main bent of post-War economics, as science and art, has been in the direction of a conscious definite abandonment of *laisser-faire* individualism, the "free" competition upon which it relied, and a purely quantitative estimate of economic costs and utilities. Everywhere governments have been compelled "by force of circumstances" to intervene in the operation of economic processes and to protect producers and consumers from the cruel consequences of commercial and industrial disasters attributable, not to the folly and incapacity of the sufferers, but to circumstances for which nobody in particular appeared to be responsible. Though these disturbances are by no means new, the magnitude of the irrationality, injustice, and inhumanity which they display has led most thoughtful men and women to abandon the notion that economic processes can best be left to work out their own salvation or damnation, and that periods of prosperity and adversity are necessary incidents of a general economic progress. Though, as we have seen, in the generation before the War a beginning had been made in the pensions, subsidies, and other "social services" for the relief of poverty and other personal disabilities, and for the provision of improved education and amenities for the "lower" classes, as well as for the better regulation of hours, wages, and other working conditions, these fragments of "Socialism" and "Communism" carried little consciousness of an organic change of policy in the relations between economics and politics. Now such organic change is clearly discernible in every civilized country, irrespective of its form of government. Dictatorships of the right or left, in Germany, Italy, Russia, and elsewhere, are busily attempting to introduce planned national unity of purpose from the political into the economic field. Its normal procedure may contain little "humanity" or equity; it is rather directed against the wastes of competitive capitalism and for a rigorous control of industry and income for military and other political ends. Its net effect may be to depress wages and to spread poverty, but security of elementary needs and of employment is an essential factor of this policy. To this extent it carries a correction of the waste of individualism and substitutes a conscious for an unconscious use of productive forces. In these States the science and the art of economics are definitely subjected to political ends.

The situation is different in countries which retain the forms and substance of political democracy, like Britain, France, America, Scandinavia. Here the lessons of post-War economic disturbance take shape in political measures of a socialistic or communistic kind designed chiefly to "humanize" industry by protecting the workers against the injuries and dangers of an economic system no longer regarded as safe, reasonable, and fair in its distribution of work and income. In fact "humanism" is coming to be regarded as the guiding principle for industry alike on its productive and consumptive side. The recognition that it is a function of the State to establish minimum wages and maximum hours is the most definite application of this principle, more "revolutionary" in its nature than any of the fragmentary nationalization of industry which is everywhere proceeding. For this public guarantee of wages and leisure strikes at the very roots of profiteering capitalism. Carried far enough, indeed, it is certain to show the general incompatibility between profiteering and humanity. For, as already appears in France and elsewhere, the attempts to recover from the consumer in higher prices the increased costs of production due to the wage and hour regulations, oblige the Government to attempt the more difficult and in many cases impossible task of regulating the selling prices. For wage-rises and increased leisure that lead to higher prices are no gain to the workers.

Though experience in this country of wage-boards in "sweated" industries shows that improved wages and other conditions of labour may induce employers to make such improvements in their methods of production as to meet the higher labour costs without a loss, this experience cannot have a general application. A policy of State-enforced humanization of private enterprises must in many cases prove impossible for the employer who is called upon to raise substantially his labour costs without the liberty to raise his selling prices. Indeed, when an industry operates largely in the world market, it is easy to perceive that any purely national policy of "humanization" along these lines is impracticable. It is the recognition of this truth that underlies the efforts of the International Labour Office to get the nations competing in world trade to agree upon simultaneous measures for shortening hours. The difficulties confronting such a "humanist" policy at present appear unsurmountable, for nations which go further than others in this direction seem likely to suffer in their export trade at a time when increases of export trade are held to be essential to recovery and progress. It is true that this may be a short-sighted view. For any damage to export trade due to rising costs of home production will to some extent be compensated out of the higher wage-incomes of the workers and the increased employment which shorter hours may bring in the essential industries. But certain British export trades would stand to suffer if their costs were raised without a similar rise of costs in their national competitors. An instance is the Lancashire cotton trade, competing over a section of its market with countries like Japan and India where labour costs are much lower. The main body of our export trade in textiles, machinery, chemicals, and coal would come under this same disability, until a reliable international co-operation, which at present seems impossible, were attained. But by many governments the substitution of a fuller intra-national trade for foreign trade is not deemed feasible. For certain foreign foods and raw materials are essential either for the maintenance of the population and its manufacturing industries, or, still more urgently at the present time, for war-materials to which all other economic considerations must be sacrificed. The new competition in armaments thus strangely interferes with the economic self-sufficiency which is a professed ideal of nationalism. Indeed, a definite clash is seen in several countries between this genuinely humanist policy and the growing demands of the "defence" services upon the national exchequer and the employment of labour. Where dictatorships or oligarchies are in control, the tendency of competitors in armaments is to absorb an increasing share of productivity, and to keep down both wages and social services to the lowest level consistent with military efficiency and popular subservience. The success which has attended the attempts to stamp out political and economic democracy in Germany, Italy, Japan, and certain other countries where it appeared to be advancing, has cast doubt upon the reality of popular power alike in the political and economic fields. In the struggle between humanism and organized force can we rely upon the victory of the former? Leaving in doubt the lasting strength of dictatorship in countries which have only tasted democracy, we may better test the issue in those countries which have had long experience of popular self-government. Here the humanist advances of the past few generations are visibly imperilled by the demands of armed defence and the sympathies for Fascism manifested by large sections of the upper classes, who prefer to undergo the expenses of armaments with the risks of war to the encroachments of a Labour or Socialist Party upon their profits and the management of industry. What I here term "humanism" appears an invasion of the rights of property to the "rentiers," the directors, the city men, the army, and the highly placed officials who see their incomes, social status, and power over their followers threatened by a "revolutionary" movement.

Whether a Fascist reaction is likely in England, France, or America turns in large measure upon the discretion of the organized democratic forces. It is not so much a matter of power as of method. This question of method applies to the ways of furthering the humanist advance successfully. Here the improvement of labour conditions goes hand in hand with the expansion and improvement of the "social services," both those which are directed to strengthening working-class family life and those which are more widely communist in character. It must, I think, be pretty clear that public aids in "social services," for education, recreation, health, and pensions, once established, cannot be withdrawn, though their enlargement and improvement may be checked.

The humanist movement in economics thus interpreted fulfils two vital purposes. As a rectification of the disordered balance between production and consumption it makes for a fuller utilization of the productive resources of a nation and reduces that pressure for external markets, alike for trade and investment, which is seen to be a main stimulus to imperialism and international competition. A better and more equitable use of the national income is thus the most valuable of peace policies. Humanism within the nation makes for humanism in the world. While it is possible that this humanism in the economic sphere may be checked in a democratic country by a war emergency and a Fascist government, nothing short of a complete defeat and subjection to a foreign Power could prevent its revival and development. Thus we see that the old economic order of virtually free private enterprise has passed away. Alike in an oligarchy and a democracy the State's relation with business has ceased to be the interference of an external body. Though some attempt is made by capitalism to keep the "planning" everywhere deemed necessary in the hands of big business men and financiers, this attempt is doomed to failure in the Fascist as in the democratic State. In other words, politics and business, after a brief spell of separation, are once more brought into organic unity. While this does not signify the disappearance of private enterprise, it does signify that all economic activities and transactions affecting human security and welfare, including national defence, will more and more come under conscious public planning. The so-called science of economics cannot under such circumstances retain its early separation from the science of politics. Therefore the tendency of economic thought must be to subordinate purely quantitative estimates of value to qualitative, the humanization of economic processes. The notorious failure of economic experts to predict the course of post-War economic events with even a moderate degree of success, has undoubtedly damaged their intellectual authority. Even upon the monetary issue involved wide differences of policy exist among the financial experts, both here and elsewhere. While, therefore, a great advance is being made in the accumulation of reliable statistics bearing upon industry and commerce, prices, incomes, credit, and other economic factors, the belief that an economic science can be built upon such a foundation finds no wide acceptance.

Public planning, whether on the part of a totalitarian State, aiming at the maximum armed strength of an economically self-sufficing nation, or of a democratic State aiming at the maximum welfare of its people, demands the liquidation of private profiteering capitalism in many important branches of production, transport, commerce, and finance, and a valuation of economic success widely divergent from any textbook reckoning. "Welfare economics," dimly and cautiously adumbrated in the economic writings of J. S. Mill, Jevons, and Marshall, have come to be recognized as superseding the older valuations, implying that wealth of an economic order must be translated into human benefits, affected alike by the nature and apportionment of its costs of production and of its utilities of consumption.* "Distribution" has thus come to be regarded as the determinant condition of these human values. Though there is no disposition to accept in its fulness the Communist formula "from each according to his ability, to each according to his needs" as a practicable rule of economic life, there is, I think, a widespread recognition that this formula expresses an ethical ideal towards which every civilized community is consciously committed. The interests of the community and of its individual members are brought into harmony by this conception of progress. For while it enlists the corporate action of government for the

* See Appendix, p. 211.

"planning" of productive activities, it safeguards the conditions of personal enjoyment and progress from the tyranny of bureaucrats or dictators. How far, how fast, and in what precise directions State Socialism with its control of key industries and its policy of "social services" shall go, will vary in each nation with the structure of its economic system, its natural and human resources, and its traditional psychology. It may well be the case that in some countries, owing to racial unity, slightness of class differences, and habits of co-operation, the sense of "fraternity" is stronger than that of individual liberty and inspires citizens to work consciously for the common good. In other countries, where class differences are strong and individual striving for personal gains and power is dominant, the domain of Socialism and State planning will be more limited and the distribution according to "needs" will be restricted in accordance with the current sentiment of "humanity." But everywhere to an increasing extent the art of economics will go more closely hand in hand with the art of politics and both will be animated more largely by a sense of the public good, whether that "good" be visualized in terms of community welfare and security, or wholly in terms of individual liberty and welfare. And with this closer conscious nexus of economic and political arts must come a corresponding nexus of their theories, as sciences. Though specialists will continue to pursue in graphs and tables the measurable facts of economic processes, the laws and theories which these measurements are designed to serve will be more and more affected by political considerations, and their right to regulate conduct in the field of industry correspondingly restricted. This signifies a radical difference between the physical and the human sciences. Whereas the former can be studied in terms of measurable facts and forces, without the intrusion of human changing thoughts and feelings, the latter cannot. No purely objective exact science of economics, politics, or ethics, is possible, and to pretend that it can be is a species of intellectual self-deceit. Whether "the good" be visualized in terms of utility, happiness, or any other form of welfare, its value is qualitative as well as quantitative, and the qualitative estimate is continually changing alike for the community and the individual. These changes, of course, are not matters of chance, the regularities or laws of this change are right objects of scientific study and of conscious direction. This is where science and art come together in the "social services." Such considerations ought to keep social students in a constant state of watchful timidity, aware that their studies can never yield "laws" on the same level of validity as the natural sciences, and that their art of prophecy must be correspondingly confined.

To argue that modern economics is moving definitely on to a welfare basis of values, alike on its cost and its utility side, that it thus seeks a reconciliation between Socialism and individualism which will avoid the disastrous wastes and perils of class conflict and international strife that proceed from unregulated capitalism, may appear to denote a personal craving on my part for a justification of my economic heresies. How far such a criticism is justified I cannot, of course, be entitled to decide, having due regard to the psychological blindness which I attribute to every owner of an intellectual property. If there be such a definite movement, as I appear to find, towards the adoption of my most cherished theses, removing them from the category of heresies, I should naturally feel some exultation, or even exaltation. It is, therefore, inherently likely that I may be mistaken in my appraisal of the new trend in economics. But I think it likely that many will admit the disappearance of the competitive capitalism which prevailed throughout most of the nineteenth century, or will think unlikely a restoration of the private profiteering enterprise in industry and commerce which formed the basis of the economic science of that epoch.

CHAPTER XII

THE WELFARE ECONOMICS OF POPULATION

THE economics of welfare has, of course, to meet the difficulty that no agreed standard of valuation for welfare on its higher levels is attainable. Whereas the growth or decline of economic wealth, reckoned in terms of money, is capable of exact measurement, the welfare related to it is not. For, as we see, it will depend upon the human costs and utilities embodied in this wealth and will vary with its distribution both in processes of production and of consumption. Nor is that the only difficulty. Our theory demands that the human values embodied in economic goods shall be "real" in the sense that they contribute to the benefit of the individual and the community as organic wholes. This consideration debars us from accepting as welfare goods which may express the mistaken immediate desire for enjoyment in disregard of the long-range organic value. Some considered conception of a human personality as a whole is evidently necessary to the right interpretation of welfare. But those who would argue that the State as representing the long-range interests of welfare of the community is alone capable of applying the organic standard go too far. For though it is true that some of the greatest benefits from an enlightened government take shape in hygienic, educational, and other measures which are in advance of the desires of most recipients of these benefits, this governmental policy must remain in fair accord with individual felt interests. If it goes strongly against private personal feelings, it will lose much of its efficacy, and will be difficult to enforce, as is seen in the case of vaccination and the abuse of alcohol.

But a more important limitation of governmental standards for ordinary economic life lies in the fact that the higher economic activities and the wealth they yield are right expressions of a personal welfare. This brings me to a final repetition of a theme which has been running throughout this economic exposition. The main economic activities of man at all times are devoted to the maintenance of those physical qualities of life in which men are similar or even identical. It is this fact that warrants the stress I lay upon the balance between routine production, ripe for Socialism, and individual production needed to satisfy those wants, needs, and desires, in which the differences of higher personality are expressed. Every man must be assumed to have a right individual estimate of his higher goods, while in his lower goods he conforms to the accepted standards of his tribe, class, or nation. When, therefore, we accredit the State experts with the right to impose certain hygienic and other practices upon producers, consumers, and citizens, we signify that the animal man, with his customary standards based on survival values, does not make adequate provision for physical or mental progress in the changing environment of his time. The supremely important issue of population comes up here. For it is here that the relation between the quantitative and the qualitative nature of wealth demands the closest consideration. For if we take Ruskin's statement "There is no wealth but life" in its most immediate meaning, all economics, politics, and ethics centre in the population question.

When Malthus opened out the issue, it appeared as a purely quantitative economic one. Population tended to outrun the means of subsistence in all countries where pestilences, famines, and wars had been got under. When after the middle of the nineteenth century restriction of the birth-rate began to cause a considerable decline in the growth of population in most Western nations, it was generally greeted with approval, although it was the expression not of a public but of a private family economy. It was held, I believe, that some real harmony existed between the family and the national policy. Parents refused to have more children than they could bring up properly and for whom they could find secure and reasonably paid employment. This natural harmony has recently been called in serious question. The peril of excessive population, as expounded by Malthus, no longer exists. The science of agriculture has to a large extent been applied so as to meet the requirements of expanding populations in most countries. The application of modern machine methods to the cultivation of the soil, and of biology to the improvement of vegetable and animal life, together with better means of communications, has made the Malthus scare appear ridiculous in countries where financial and other public measures are being taken to curb the excessive productivity of crops and herds.

The scare has turned from an excessive to a deficient birth-rate. In some countries the declining birth-rate is held to carry grave dangers. At the present rate of decline our population will have almost disappeared in another century. The same holds true of France and certain other civilized countries. Even in our Dominions a serious decline is taking place. It is quite true that in Russia, China, India, and parts of Africa the population, less subject to the "natural checks" by reason of improved knowledge and communications, is growing rapidly. But this is no consolation to the Western nations, for it seems to them to imply a disappearance of civilization as they know and value it, and the peopling of the earth by definitely lower races. Some advanced nations are endeavouring to encourage earlier marriages and larger families by subsidies, tax reliefs, and other public benefits. Their motives for this encouragement of population are mixed. In the case of France, Germany, Italy, and Russia, military considerations rank high. Cannon fodder is needed for defensive or offensive warfare, more workers for the armament industries and for national self-sufficiency of life. This military purpose is associated with a pride of race and a policy of territorial expansion which calls for a higher birth-rate to give it validity. Germany, Italy, and Japan prize a growing population, partly as a pretext for, partly as an instrument of, territorial expansion. This pride of race must not, however, be regarded as a mere display of national egotism. It opens up the large new issue of qualitative population. That issue is obscured when a purely economic view of a population is taken. A good deal of attention has recently been given to the term "optimum" population interpreted as meaning that population which can make the fullest use of the productive resources of a given area of land, yielding the highest economic income. Equally distributed according to needs, such a maximum production would, it is maintained, imply the largest amount of economic welfare. If a world economy could be managed on this basis, by a distribution of productive population in accordance with the natural resources of each country, it would appear to some that the problem of population would be solved. And so it would, on two assumptions, that "economic goods" constituted the sole measure of human welfare, and that all stocks and races of men were equally desirable from the standpoint of human value.

But neither of these assumptions can be readily admitted. Average or maximum economic productivity cannot be taken as a sufficient criterion of a desirable life. Two considerations debar it. From the standpoint of human economics, it may be better to produce a volume of goods below the "optimum" if thereby the human costs of production are reduced. Most populational "optimists" do not take into account costs of production but only utilities of consumption. This consideration of costs, however, is closely linked with that of leisure and the whole range of non-economic factors in human welfare. The importance of leisure, as we realize, grows greater with every increased mechanization and standardization of work. But though, in a sense, this leisure is itself an economic product, its translation into desirable and beneficial modes of living belongs to free personality and lies outside the field of "optimum productivity." Some uses of leisure will, of course, produce high forms of economic goods but other uses will yield vital values so individually qualitative as to negate comparison. My whole argument is that the economic system in a progressive civilized society forms the basis of a higher personal and communal life whose values evade strict measurement.

But are all people to be deemed equally capable of these intrinsically higher vital values? If they are, then the economic problem seems soluble on the basis of such distribution of work and wealth as will give equal leisure and liberty of personal growth to all. But if they are not equal, does not our conception of maximum human welfare require us to take account of this inequality? Here we encounter two widely divergent views. Most members of civilized countries believe that their national and racial population is superior in mental, moral, and other cultural values to the peoples of the backward countries, and in a less degree to the peoples of other civilized countries. "We are the best people" seems a natural sentiment for patriots. It is certainly the valuation of Britons, Americans, Frenchmen, Germans, Italians, and the Russians of to-day. If, therefore, an "optimum" population for the world is to be an avowed aim for a world policy, these self-declared superiorities of nation and race must be taken into account. But such a theoretic accountancy is not either feasible or logically defensible. Such sense of national or racial supremacy may be natural, but it cannot be taken as a disinterested judgment. But are we, therefore, to deny that any inherent superiority of human values attaches to any or all of the civilized white peoples, and that it matters nothing if they decline in population and are displaced by the more prolific populations of Asia and Africa? Even the minority of thinkers who are persuaded that no inherent differences of racial values exist and that all the higher qualities of civilized life are due to differences of environment and education, would have to admit that these differences require a considerable time for their beneficial operation, and that a rapid decline of the more civilized peoples could not be compensated immediately by the fuller opportunities afforded to migrants from the backward countries. So far as the superiority of climatic and other factors of physical environment are responsible for the physical and mental calibre of civilized peoples, it is quite evident that a rapid decline of population would be accompanied by a loss of values in the higher realms of human activity. We are not, therefore, called upon to decide whether any inherent or acquired transmissible superiority attaches to this or that civilized people. If we assumed that all were sons of Adam and that no distinct origins for primitive man were available, the long impress of certain physical environments with their cultural traditions must count so heavily as to disable us from regarding with indifference the decline of Western populations.

A not less crucial issue has arisen within the population of each country. Birth-restriction, as practised in this country, and to a less extent elsewhere, has been selection in what is held to be a wrong direction. Statistics show that the earlier exercise of birth control was confined to the better informed and more intelligent classes whose birth-rate, even when better survival conditions were taken into account, was definitely below that of the working classes. Though in recent times popular instruction has expanded the area of birth control so as to include large sections of the workers, it still remains true that the reproduction rate of the upper grades is less than that of the lower grades of the population. Here again comes up the question of "stock" within each national area. Is some stock inherently superior, or is it merely a question of equality of opportunity, of material and cultural environment? Though by sympathy a keen environmentalist, I have never been able to get rid of the belief that heredity counts heavily, not merely for "success" in life, but for the higher intellectual and creative values. It is not merely the patent instances of families so rich in genius and ability as the Darwins, Huxleys, Coleridges, but my general experience of hereditary talent on a less distinguished level that obliges me to the conviction that our output of the highest values is seriously impaired by the small or no families of most of the men and women of greatest intellectual distinction in my time. It may well be the case (I have often argued it) that no approach towards equality of educational opportunities yet exists, and that only a small proportion of the naturally gifted sons and daughters of the poorer classes can avail themselves of those opportunities which are wrongly supposed to be within their reach. But while this is a strong argument in favour of a genuine equalization of educational and other opportunities, it does not dispose of the refusal of many men and women of genius or high capacity to realize the duty of transmitting such qualities as experience shows to be transmissible.

It may be true, as is sometimes maintained, that not only the desire but the capacity of procreation weakens as man rises from a purely animal existence to a higher intellectual and emotional life. It may also be the case that the bearing and rearing of children conflict with the exercise of the new activities to which the more intellectual women are addicted. The equalitarianism, political and economic, which has displaced male supremacy, alike in the home and outside of it, has probably brought some contempt for the child-bearing and rearing functions among many active-minded women. If education and environment were everything, this might not count for much and might be compensated by the spread of opportunities among the "lower" classes. But if transmissible superior qualities of stock and race are important contributions to human worth, a situation, like the present, in which lower stocks and lower races displace higher stocks and higher races would denote a human retrogression. It may be that the conscious organized movement towards security of family livelihood, which is playing an important part in the public policy of most advanced peoples, will do much to reduce the risks and costs of larger families and to restore the natural appeal of child-life to married people. If it is possible for a newly married couple to have both a baby and a motor-car without injury to their accepted ways of living, the car may cease to oust the baby.

One final consideration, not easily assessable, should enter into any treatment of the population questions.

If it be true that human life in general, with all its chances and changes, its successes and failures, is desired and desirable, the quantitative aspect of the population question has a proper and perhaps an important place in any economy of human welfare. This consideration may override the purely economic test of an optimum. For it may be better to have a larger number of human beings living somewhat below that higher economic level which our "optimists" desiderate, provided the lower level makes an adequate provision for the prime needs of life. Setting aside the philosophy of pessimism, the mere fact that nearly everyone prefers to go on living is *prima facie* evidence that life as such is a positive value. How valuable nobody is in a position to judge, but if it be held to have some value, then the larger the population the larger the volume of that value. Though this inherent value of life is admittedly dependent upon a sufficiency of food and other material economic goods, it cannot rightly be measured by the monetary or even the utility value of these goods. For the end or result may be immeasurably, i.e. qualitatively, more valuable than the means. Not a few civilized persons who have lived among primitive peoples, well accommodated to their environment, put a higher value upon their lot than upon the life of the modern cities in which most civilized people live on a higher economic level. There is, doubtless, a great deal of the "artificial," or mere "swank" in civilization, and some measure of "return to nature" in a simpler human life may not only be desirable, but come to be desired. To not a few of us, the recent rush of the fine arts and literature into fantastic eccentricity and flamboyancy attests a failure in that higher self-command which is the supreme quality of personality. There are, of course, grave perils to our material civilization from the failure of pacific co-operation in the political and economic fields. But a collapse of those creative arts of thought and imagination, hitherto regarded as the supreme achievements of man, would, it is contended, complete the human downfall. How much truth attaches to these abuses of science and the fine arts it is difficult for those of us who are unskilled in any of those activities to judge. It may well be the case that the fears I cite arise from the hasty judgments of persons predisposed to hostile criticism of matters of which they are conscious of possessing little knowledge. After all, the long range of history discloses not a few epochs when the rapid advances of science and novelties in literature and the fine arts have evoked fears and condemnations as terrifying as those that to-day fill the minds of some intellectual agitators. Is it fair to describe the science of our time as primarily subservient to the arts of physical destruction, or our fine arts as devoted to the cult of ugliness and inhumanity?

CHAPTER XIII

WESTERN CHRISTIANITY

In any attempt to estimate the rise or decline of human values, it is, of course, necessary to take due account of the reputed decay of religious faith and feelings. Here we are on a wider field than in dealing with the sciences and arts. So far as religion is concerned with dogmatic creeds and ceremonial, there can be no question that the Churches have lost much of their former hold on their adherents. This is, as I have already intimated, due not so much to any conscious scepticism as to a growing sense of the unreality of any other world and any other life than this. For how many church-goers to-day has the doctrine of Atonement any meaning? How many believe in the "saving" of their souls? "The exceeding Sinfulness of Sin," "Righteousness," the "grace of God" carry little emotional appeal. As for miracles, perhaps it would be right to say that the miracles of another world have been displaced by the miracles of this world. To the mass of people in civilized countries the interest of ordinary life, outside the routine of work, has been immensely enlarged. Perhaps "sport" and its accompaniments have done as much as anything to absorb the lighter interest of most men in all classes of society in this country and America, and its spread to most continental countries has helped to concentrate attention upon the physical activities of man. But there is a deeper reason for the failure of Christianity in its insistent attempts to foist on to Western nations that are distinctively materialistic, combative, and individualistic, in their real aims and interests, ideals of character and conduct out of keeping with their nature and traditions. The teaching of the Sermon on the Mount is so evidently divergent from our real feelings about men and women's characters and conduct as to drive its teachers to all sorts of evasive interpretations. It is not a question of gradual spiritual advances towards the adoption of the Christian teaching. The character of Jesus, though commanding a conventional respect and even admiration, is not the ideal character of an English gentleman, an English sportsman,* or an English business man, an English scholar, even an English clergyman. The full Christian

* Many of the best qualities of Englishmen are educated in their sporting activities. It was not merely "courage" that was implied in the oft-quoted statement that "Waterloo was won in the playing fields of Eton." The sporting spirit which is widespread among all classes has no doubt spread by quasi-snobbish adoption of the behaviour and standards of the gentry. It carries, however, many fine and even elevated rules of conduct. Justice is "fair play," love of neighbours is the "team spirit," and although "love of enemies" cannot be recognized, there is at least tolerance for rival teams and some appreciation of their virtues as gamesters. I quote an illuminating sentence from a work of fiction by the Rev. Ronald A. Knox: "I love that phrase, don't you, *playing the game*. The pill of morality coated with sporting metaphor, so that the English can take it without difficulty!" (*Double Cross Purposes*, p. 283).

character is inherently and eternally alien from Western civilized man, his valuations and his ideals. Some recognition of this truth is discernible in the Aryan-Christianity by which the Nazis seek to pour the substance of their barbaric faith into the emptied shell of the Christian creed.

But it is not necessary for us to go so far as the Nazis in repudiating the ethics of Christianity. All we have to do is to refuse to recognize that Christ's ethics in the Sermon on the Mount and elsewhere have any application to modern social institutions. These are purely personal ethics. The Christian Churches must, therefore, keep out of politics and economics, for "The Church has its own message to deliver, a message which it cannot deliver if it mingles in political agitations." "The plain truth is that power is always abused, and that the masses, who now have the power, and are morally neither better nor worse than the upper and middle classes whom they have supplanted, intend to pillage the minority for their own benefit."*

"There is nothing contrary to the Gospel or to Christian principles in collective experiments which do not involve confiscation." But Dr. Inge plainly regards the "power politics" of the masses as pillage and confiscation anti-Christian practices. "The revolutionary creed flatly contradicts Christianity at every point." The repudiation of Religion by Marx

* Dr. Inge, *Christian Ethics and Modern Problems*, pp. 38, 90.

and Lenin is sufficient for him. "The real function of the Church is to hold up steadily before both the conflicting forces the Christian standard of values."* But it is evident that the Christian Churches must side with the owning classes in opposing as "revolutionary" any serious attempt of a democracy to reform the distribution of wealth. Everywhere the Christian Churches are found ranging themselves with the "Conservative classes," and this sight everywhere saps their influence among the class-conscious workers. This does not imply a condemnation of the Churches for failure to carry out a social ethics of Christianity, but simply a recognition that the Churches belong to the "established order" and confer a certain sacredness on their cause.† The coincidence of Protestantism with the rise of modern capitalism was no accident of history. Capitalism could not have found its necessary freedom under the dominion which the Romish Church exercised over the conduct of secular life. Its prohibition of usury, its principle of a fair price, its claim to regulate on spiritual rules the processes of bargaining and markets, though punctured by various evasions and exceptions, were hostile to the free play of capitalist industry, commerce, and finance. The removal of Papal authority from the

* Dr. Inge, *Christian Ethics and Modern Problems,* p. 391.

† R. H. Tawney's *Religion and the Rise of Capitalism* is the most useful study of the more positive contribution of Protestantism to the support of modern industrialism.

secular processes was, therefore, a great stimulus to liberty of production, trade, and human intercourse. But this liberation was not the only service rendered by Protestantism. It had a more positive contribution in the value its Churches set upon certain economic virtues which were needed to promote successful business. In particular industry, honesty (the best policy), and thrift from sober living, gave a spiritual sanction to successful business, and incidentally assisted to promote co-operation for profitable business ends. But upon the whole Protestantism made for the dissociation of the religious from the secular life, the weekday ethics from the Sabbath, and as time went on reduced religion to a set of ideals, rules, and dogmas which had less and less reality in the ordinary ways of men. The Sunday parade of the Sermon on the Mount is regarded by most Christians to-day as a beautiful ethic which has no real application to any department of secular conduct.

But while the full substance of this Eastern faith is now widely recognized as impracticable for an operative principle in the Western world, whether Catholic or Protestant in profession, it is not right to conclude that religion in its broader spiritual and philosophic sense is disappearing or weakening. If religion be taken to signify man's emotional concern for his life as a moral and rational personality in an ever enlarging human society, and his interest in the discovery of an order in the Universe, to which man by the use of his conscious faculties may contribute, such a religion is gradually but certainly growing, not only among the sensitive and intellectual minorities of each people, but as a pervasive and as yet half-conscious motive in the minds of the many. This may seem a doubtful statement and perhaps inconsistent with the dominance attributed to the lighter interests, but I hold it to be supported by the widespread and various aspects of the humanist movement. Though this movement may appear to be eclipsed temporarily by a brutalitarian movement in some European countries, a wider survey of the past few centuries will show a remarkable development of man's concern for his neighbours' welfare and an expansion of the term neighbour, checked but not lastingly defeated by the appeals of Nationalism.

Although the more definitely philosophic aspect of religion concerned with man's place in the Universe may not seem to be making a corresponding advance, that is because of the too conventional view of philosophy. Popular education to-day, not so much in the schools as in the general experiences of life, is rapidly transforming the ordinary man's view of man, both in relation to other animals and to his general physical and moral environment. Man no longer stands alone, separate in structure and in vital qualities from his surroundings: he is simply the highest present product of powers which permeate the universe and inspire in various combinations and degrees all the creatures and events which constitute that universe. As his knowledge of that universe is enlarged by science or by ordinary experience, he comes to feel a closer kinship with his non-human as well as his human surroundings. It is that sense of kinship that gives new substance to our modern religion with its double significance for humanity, first as the co-operative body of human beings, secondly as the corporate part of a system inspired and moulded by some evolving process that may be realized as purpose or even spirit. For the nineteenth-century scientific rejection of purposes or spiritual hypotheses was clearly overdone. Among our leading scientists and philosophers there is little of that pride of intellectual self-sufficiency so blatant in mid- or late-Victorian times. Many of them admit some other faculty than reason as a means of getting truth. Materialism, Determinism, Rationalism are all discarded as inadequate instruments for reaching the highest realms of truth and for explaining the nature of a changing world.* Modern analyses of the mental processes which even mathematicians undergo in reaching new "laws" indicate the operation of some creative imagination that goes beyond their accumulated knowledge and is akin to intuition. Indeed, in a world where history never repeats itself exactly but

* C. Delisle Burns in *Horizons of Experience* gives a masterly survey of this view of Evolution as applied to the different arts of life.

always takes on some new and unknown factor, it is impossible to rely wholly upon the laws that can only generalize our past experiences. Evolution is no longer taken to signify the smooth unfolding of back urges in causation, but admits the play of movements and events in front as well as those behind.

Without some such theory in our mind, it is impossible to seek to understand or to evaluate the many unexpected changes of human conduct and values in the ambit of economics, politics, ethics, religion, philosophy which I have cited here. History has shown other epochs marked by changes as wonderful and as various in their significance. But none of the earlier changes has been so startling in its revelation of the possible contribution of science to the latent brutality of man as disclosed in modern arts and deeds of destruction.

In his old age, some time before the rise of Nazism and Fascism, Lord Bryce came to doubt the triumph of democracy as a principle of government. His arresting phrase, "Another ice age may be settling down upon the human mind," goes even deeper into the nature of "our present discontents," for it suggests a decline of those human qualities, interests, passions, and abilities which are summed up in the term "progress of humanity."

On the other hand, may not this peril be exaggerated in the minds of the old among us by a lifelong belief in the growth of reason and humanity which appeared to be making progress not only on the material plane but in the arts of personal conduct and of government? Events which seem to carry a shattering of this faith may be arousing a sudden panic in our aged breasts. But if our lifelong sense of progress has found support in so many centuries of intellectual and moral advancement, it seems inherently unlikely that a few years' debauch of folly and of hate can permanently reverse the course of human history and plunge us back to barbarism.

CHAPTER XIV

AN ECONOMIC JOURNEY TOWARDS HUMANISM

If one gets away from the economics of the market in which money is the measure of work and wealth into the economics of human values, one is inevitably drawn into what may appear to be "the jumble" of politics, ethics, art, religion, which constitutes the setting of my thought. My main endeavour, however, has been to show that though the human treatment of economic activities links up with all these other activities, they do not form a "jumble" but a moving harmony of relations, in which the several values, though capable of separate study, must finally be seen as contributory factors in the art of living. I cannot pretend that my development of this thesis has been an orderly continuous intellectual journey. Far from it. My earliest statement of the over-saving heresy was a quarrel with orthodoxy within the range of quantitative economic science. It was only later on that it led me to a closer analysis of the bargaining processes in the markets for goods and productive services which disclosed the inequalities of income that gave rise to "over-saving" and the waste it brought about in periods of depression. An almost chance excursion into the field of imperialist enterprise in South Africa brought me to perceive and trace the intimate causal relations between a rate of saving excessive for home purposes and the drive for the exploitation of backward countries which is the economic core of imperialism. Thus I was launched upon two different yet not unrelated theses, a distinctively moral criticism of that bargaining process which is the core of distribution, and an equally distinctive political activity in which the profiteering motive played a determinant part.

In most of my closer reasoning my prime concern has been to give a consistent intelligible account of the bargaining process, so as to bring the "laws" of wages, rent, interest, and profit on to the same plane of statement. I found a law of rent, representing it as differential payments from a no-rent margin, which ignored the patent fact that for most uses of land the margin carried a positive rental. I found a law of wages that ignored the difference between the subsistence or replacement payment which counts in dealing with capital and land, and the positive wage-payment. I found a treatment of capital and interest which regarded them not as concrete factors in production, but as monetary figures. I found profit entirely vague in its origin and nature, sometimes including wages of management, costs of risk-taking, interest of capital, gains from profiteering, and what not. I cannot profess complete success in my attempt (in *Distribution of Wealth*) to put these different sources of income on a single consistent footing. Even had my logic been accurate, the customary attitudes and language of the business world would have presented insurmountable obstacles. But I claim to have done something towards the establishment of a consistent conception of supply and demand and market, applicable to all kinds of goods and services, productive or consumptive. This conception of market played a central rôle in all my later economic thinking. For it enabled me to resolve the supplies and demands of all concrete goods and services into costs and utilities reckoned in terms of human value, i.e. costs expressing painful or injurious experiences, utilities expressing pleasurable or beneficial experiences. This line of analysis led me to present economics in a distinctively qualitative character. For though concrete supplies and demands of goods and services and their prices still were reckoned in quantities, their human costs and utilities varied with the qualities of the persons who bore those costs or enjoyed those utilities. The issue of the apportionment of concrete costs and utilities among the different sexes and ages, capacities, and defects, of the producing and consuming population, stood out as of prime importance in reckoning the human value of any change of industrial processes or of standards of living. Thus, though an increase in the quantity of goods, turned out by improved technique, carried *prima facie* an increase in the means of enjoyment, both the amount and the nature of that increase depended upon the distribution of its human costs and utilities among the participants.

This question of distribution kept me continually busy in examining the markets from the standpoint of the bargaining strength of the sellers and buyers. For it became ever more evident that the free competition among producers which was the virtual guarantee of common benefit according to the *laisser-faire* economics, was declining in many markets, and was destined to give place to various forms and degrees of monopoly. My American studies threw strong light upon this issue, making it clear that in a mainly self-contained community, with little political interference with business enterprise and no effective public support to the weaker workers and consumers, the economic system must become increasingly subject to centralized financial controls and to a regulation of outputs that would greatly restrict the productivity of capitalism. Wild plunges into foreign loans and investments, followed by sudden withdrawals, equally wild plunges into gambling speculations at home, and a temporary closing down of employment in almost all occupations, followed by a revival due to immense expenditures on public works, public loans, and subsidies and armaments—this recent amazing exhibition of economic events in America brings home to intelligent observers everywhere the conviction that there is something seriously wrong with capitalism as seen in the biggest and richest country where it has had the freest play.

In every other country capitalism, competitive and monopolistic, displays the same defects and applies similar political and economic remedies in order to save its life from the new revolutionary attacks of socialism and communism. Regarded more narrowly from my own standpoint of criticism, what has occurred is a display and condemnation of the unequal and unfair character of all markets. For nowhere are the bargaining powers of supply and demand on an equal footing, and everywhere the individual buyers and sellers, whether of goods or services, are so unequal in their "need" to sell and buy that the advantage accruing from sales at any given price give widely different advantages to those who participate. In other words, whether under monopoly or so-called competitive conditions, markets are intrinsically unfair modes of distribution.

This is my most destructive heresy, and therefore the one for which I have least succeeded in gaining attention, even in the form of hostile criticism, from the orthodox economists. The defence of capitalism consists mainly in ignoring positive attacks and in concentrating upon the errors, follies, and divided counsels of its assailants. Among the business and professional classes and their economic supporters the conviction holds that any property or income legally acquired represents the productive services rendered by its recipient, either in the way of skilled brain or hand work, thrift, risks, or enterprise, or as inheritance from one who has thus earned it. The notion that any such property or income can contain any payment which is excessive, or the product of superior bargaining power, never enters their minds. Writers to *The Times*, protesting against a rise in the Income Tax, always speak of their "right" to the income they have "made," and regard any tax as a grudging concession to the needs of an outsider, the State.

So long as this belief prevails all serious attempts by a democracy to set the production and distribution of income upon an equitable footing will continue to be met by the organized resistance of the owning classes, which, if they lose control of the political machinery, will not hesitate to turn to other methods of protecting their "rights."

It would be foolish for me to pretend that my human interpretation of cost and utility, and economic value has not led me into serious intellectual difficulties. With these difficulties I have sought to cope in several of my later books. So long as economics concerned itself exclusively with saleable goods and services, it could be kept separate from non-economic activities and values. But my interpretation in human terms brings economic values into close organic relations with other human values. Man is seen as an organism all activities of which are interdependent. The good or bad results of economic activities must react upon the values of other activities. The simplest instance, of course, is the effect of the nature and duration of the working day upon the uses of leisure. But, when we regard man as an organic unity, we perceive that each of his non-economic activities, his play, his politics, his home life, his reading, etc., must react both upon his economic activities and upon the specific costs and utilities that appertain to them. Such intricate interactions evidently preclude much of the specialism and separatism which economic, political, and other social theorists have been prone to claim for the study to which they devote themselves. The organic nature of man, as person and member of a society, requires that each result of a special social study in a particular field shall continually be submitted for its appraisal to the wider survey of all human values. It is perhaps unlikely that this statement will be denied. But the whole trend of orthodox economics has been to safeguard economic practices from submission to such a general survey of human values. This is the real meaning of the attempt to keep economics within the limits of the quantitative measurements of markets, and to prevent the intrusion of ethical considerations into its field. The failure of this strictly quantitative science is due, as we have seen, not so much to its intellectual weakness, as to the recent political and humanist invasions into large fields of business arising from the failure of planless industry, commerce, and finance to "deliver the goods." The "planning" under which capitalists seek to establish or retain their economic control involves a multifarious co-operation between politics and economics, with "ethics" for the protection of the weak producer and the weak consumer and for the furtherance of "social services." The current struggle in the surviving "democratic" countries is between this reformed capitalism, figuring as disinterested expertism, and a governmental control representing the popular interests and will. Reformed capitalism will make strictly necessary concessions in the way of limitations upon profits, collective bargaining with labour, minimum wages and maximum hours, representation of workers and consumers upon joint boards, provided that the substance of the financial and business management is left in their hands with the opportunities of profit which it affords.

Economic Democracy demands something more and something different. It demands that the whole of economic life shall be brought under a planning based on a conception of a desirable human life as interpreted and administered by the popular will through the instrument of Government. This view, however, as I take it, does not imply a rigorous control by the State over the whole body of economic processes. The main purport of my latest reasoning has been to apply to State socialism certain limitations derived from the view that men are both alike and different in their organic make-up of body and mind, and that this likeness and difference should be reflected properly in the organization of industry.

So far as men are alike in their make-up their

economic needs will be the same, and can best be met by standardized planning. Such planning inhibits competitive enterprise and is essentially monopolistic. But these monopolies cannot be left to privately owned businesses to determine the regulation of output and prices. They form the natural substance of municipal or national (ultimately international) socialism. In most countries the standard services for the supply of communications, postal, telegraphic, telephonic, aerial; transport, by roads, rail, sea, air; power, light, heat, and their sources, mines, electricity, water; iron, steel, timber, and other staple materials; money and banking facilities, are in large measure under public ownership and operation. What everyone needs can best be supplied by large publicly ordered services free from the waste of competition or of profiteering. That is the economic principle. If it involves some bureaucratic defects, these must be set against the merits of a secure, honest, standardized service. One qualification, however, must be taken into account. The full economy of standardization depends not only upon identity in human needs, but also upon identity in the materials used in industry for the satisfaction of those needs. In some cases that identity is lacking. Even in the services for the supply of routine goods the standardization of the productive processes may be interfered with by the differences of shape or quality of some essential raw material or in the method of producing it. Wherever such raw material is of an organic nature there is some waste involved in treating it as identical in quality and structure. The great examples, of course, lie in agriculture. Where large areas of land are similar in soil, climate, situation, accessibility to markets, such slight differences as exist in growing crops or raising animals may be disregarded in favour of the economics of co-operative or State farming. But in a country like England or parts of France where each small field presents a business proposition of its own, the amount of mechanized working through co-operative action may be strictly limited, and from the standpoint of largest and best outputs it may be a better economy to leave the control of the ordinary farming processes to owners or tenants with some pecuniary inducement in the shape of profit. The supply of biological information regarding crops and animals, the supply of tractors and other expensive machinery, of information regarding markets, the organization of marketing processes—in such ways the State can render assistance to agriculture without "socializing" it. If it be contended that public control of an adequate secure supply of primary foods is essential, this may best be secured by subsidies and other modes of financial regulation.

But important as this exception may be, it does not interfere with the truth that socialism must take control of the productive processes that supply the ordinary standard needs of human beings. This economy will soon extend to the supply of many comforts and even luxuries where by convention or imitation the demand is closely standardized. Alcohol and tobacco are State-owned or State-controlled industries in many countries. But since such "needs" cannot be regarded as based on common physiological needs, they will tend to vary with differences of taste and fashion and will not furnish a steady or calculable market. Most of them form a legitimate field for private profitable risk-taking adventure, in which the freedom of the producer matches the caprice of the customer.

But it will be generally recognized that socialism is not to be confined to planning secure and abundant supplies of goods to satisfy the primary personal needs of the animal man, or even his essential needs. It has another function. That is to supply those services of health, education, insurance, pensions which lie outside the knowledge and the capacity of their personal beneficiaries, and which are large contributions towards the welfare of the community. Few will deny that these conditions of stability and progress are essential to the enlargement of liberty and opportunity for ordinary men and women, and help towards a realization of the values of personality. Holding, as I do, that the life of a community is something other than the mere addition of the life of its members, I see in such "socialism" an enlargement and enrichment of the common life.

CHAPTER XV

THE REVISION OF DEMOCRACY

It is pretty evident that our conception of the right relations between politics and economics will oblige us to discard a good deal of the vague idealism and semi-mysticism which grew round the nineteenth-century conception of democracy.* So long as politics

* To Carlyle and Ruskin the domination of the Master in politics, as in business life, seemed inevitable and desirable. They were to be "humanized" in the sense of having due regard for the welfare (as they saw it) of those placed under their charge. But no question of interfering with their Captainship could arise. Parliament was a somewhat contemptible "talking shop," useful, if at all, in letting off steam. Carlyle, however, did not go so far as Nietzsche in regarding democracy as "a breeding ground for Tyrants." Nietzsche's prophecy, uttered in 1886, deserves citation. "The birth of the European may be delayed. The march of events that is bringing this to pass may slow down, may suffer relapses, gaining thereby in vehemence and depth: one such relapse will come from the still raging storms of frantic nationalism. I think the results of this process will be such as utterly to confound all the naïve advocates of 'progress,' the apostles of 'modern ideas.' These new conditions of life, calculated to level man down to an equal mediocrity—to produce a useful, industrious, herd-animal type of human being, easily employable for all sorts of purposes—are peculiarly likely to give birth to a few exceptional men of most dangerous and fascinating quality. While the general type of the future European will be that of the garrulous, will-less, extraordinarily suggestible worker, who needs an employer to give him orders as he needs his daily bread, here and there we shall see the strong man becoming stronger and more talented than ever—

and economics were kept separate in thought and practice, it seemed easy to envisage a popular will expressing itself in electioneering processes and aiming at some generalized equality of opportunities in a freely competitive order of society. But as soon as equality of opportunities was subjected to closer analysis and the adjective "economic" was firmly applied to opportunities, it became evident that political democracy was almost empty of value without economic democracy in the sense of equal access to the use of all the factors of production and to the products of their co-operation.

Put in its popular appeal, economic democracy implied that labour was no longer to be the servant of those who owned the land and tools, power and finance, and the expert knowledge relating to their use, but that it was to be recognized as the creative agent in all productive processes and the rightful claimant to the wealth produced. Though, as we have seen, this popular appeal requires some important qualifications in view of high forms of productive skill and energy, not commonly classed as "labour," its emergence as a source of political reform, and of a true conception of democracy needs to be taken into serious account. If it remains in its crude form, a

thanks to the lack of traditions and prejudices, and to the immense variety of the environment in which he has been brought up. My belief is that democratized Europe will turn out to be a training-school and a breeding-ground for Tyrants, in every sense of the word."

denial of all rights of property to inventiveness, risk-taking adventure, organization and direction of industry, trade, and finance, it makes for a class-war within each nation and for international war between democracies envisaged as communist and those fascist States that fear a reversal of their dictatorship.

The setting of Democracy upon a sound, equitable, and workable footing is the only escape from this class and international war. And this escape can only be achieved by incorporating right modes of economic rule in the art of government. The crude principle of a distinctively political democracy in which all men, irrespective of their wide differences in ability, character, and experience are supposed to count equally through the franchise and the representative system, cannot figure as the right principle for economic democracy. The determinant policy in each of the productive arts must be vested in a minority of trained specialized brain and hand workers who understand how to perform the several related operations. The delicate work of correlating the various industries, distinguishing those closely dependent on one another from those that run productive courses of their own, providing the due proportions of the different sorts of capital and labour among them and settling the necessary rates of pay to evoke the best productive efforts for each sort of service—such skilled expert direction must evidently be vested in men of special competence. The mass opinion of producer-consumers in their capacity of localized voters cannot be vested with any power to overrule such expert control. Where, then, does the democratic principle or policy come in? I think that our organic distinction between standardized and free enterprise helps towards an answer to this important question. In standardized industries where most productive work is narrow, dull, and costly to its performers, there is an evident need of trade-union organization to safeguard the ordinary worker against the undue pressure of skilled managers looking too closely at increased outputs and low labour costs. This safeguard should have constitutional recognition through joint councils of managers and workers, with appeals to a general board of conciliation on which employers and employees of other industries, together with representatives of the consuming public, should sit and whose judgments should have legal force. For since all these standardized processes, involving human costs, are directed to the satisfaction of the primary needs of consumers, it is clear that consumers must have some real control over the qualities and quantities of the output of these industries. Consumers' co-operative societies may usefully contribute to the essential task of economic democracy, bringing more expert knowledge to bear than can be got from the unorganized individual consumers.* Indeed, it is neces-

* Perhaps the most valuable recent experimentation in a varied programme of economic reform, where social legislation, State

sary to the best working of this socialism that an effective protection and instruction be afforded by the consumer public against the misdirection of standard industries by rulers primarily devoted to the efficient organization of the productive processes. The citizen-consumer must have such protection against loss of his liberty of choice in the realm of socialized industries. If our distinction between standardized and free industries be accepted, he will exercise a direct and personal control over the free industries which furnish him with goods and services expressive of his separate personal needs. This combination of socialized standardized industries and individual private enterprise will need expression in a combined political and economic government. For it is evident that the free private enterprise will require the protection of political government and will have financial and other obligations to that government. In other words, I envisage an economic democracy in which the socialization of standardized and key industries, voluntary co-operative enterprise, and private business enterprise will perform different sorts of productive work, while the consumers' final interests and liberties must be secured through the ordinary forms of popular local elections, supplemented by participation in concilia-

control of public utilities, and co-operation go hand in hand, is furnished by Sweden and Denmark. The story of Sweden is told in an excellent way by Marquis W. Childs, in a book entitled *Sweden, the Middle Way*, published by the Yale University Press (1936).

tion and arbitration boards dealing with specific industrial problems.

The working out of these problems may involve changes in the political modes of democracy. For a visible defect in the working of political democracy, concerned as it is with non-economic as well as economic issues, and with foreign as well as domestic policy, is disclosed by the high measure of economic specialism in certain electoral areas. In purely agricultural districts, in mining areas, in cotton or other textile centres, in some machinery and shipping centres, the predominance of certain producing groups in the electioneering processes tends to pack the House of Commons with members representative primarily of these specialized trades, to which the wider interests of the country and issues of foreign policy are wholly subsidiary. Here narrow forces of economic democracy damage the general operation of political democracy. New problems of the Special Areas, of local claims to industrial subsidies are thus added to the protective measures by which this country, like many others, seeks to secure economic self-sufficiency by control of external trade.

I can make no pretence to offering a practical solution of these electoral problems. It must here suffice to point out that the increasing pressure of important economic issues upon a democratic machinery which had been framed without regard to them, renders obligatory an early radical readjustment in the instruments of political democracy and their operation, if democracy is to escape the sham dictatorship of the proletariat on the one hand, the real dictatorship of a Fascist capitalism upon the other.

It has seemed to some that the recent experiment in a National Government in Great Britain is at least one step towards the achievement of such a democracy. Since it is claimed that all parties are represented in this Government it might appear to be better suited for the performance of the new economic functions than a Government based on a single party of the "right" or "left," with an Opposition which adopted the traditional attitude of the former party system. But such a claim cannot bear close inspection. For the balance of representation in this National Government clearly indicates that, while holding a formal middle place between continental Fascism and Communism, it is in reality a defence of property Government, occupied with the "concession" policy at home and abroad, deemed appropriate to this defensive rôle. If we are to achieve the substance of economic democracy, it must come through what I would call the rationalization of the Labour Party, involving an adoption of some such middle policy of socialism as is here adumbrated, and the dropping of the crude conception of political democracy formed during the revolutionary era in favour of one which embodies the expert requirements of economic democracy.

This issue has shown itself recently in the discord within the Labour Party. The trade unions, whose members constitute a majority of organized labour, whose contributions form the chief source of party finance, and whose votes determine the candidature and the election to Parliament of most Labour members, are not socialist in their interests, aims, and policies, except in the sense that they seek to utilize the State to strengthen their bargaining power with Capital by means of legal minimum wages, hours, and other "conditions," and by the provision of "social services." Now this is not socialism in the sense in which that policy is understood by most members of the Left organizations and most members of the constituency groups. That socialism aims primarily at the substitution of public ownership and control over capitalist enterprise in all key and fundamental industries, and the elimination of unearned incomes from the economic system. The difference is deep and genuine between the worker-citizens concerned chiefly or entirely with the betterment of the economic conditions of their particular trade, local or national, and those concerned with the promotion by political action of the economic welfare of the whole community.

While a few of this latter group hold seats in Parliament and succeed in some measure in imposing their socialistic designs upon the more receptive of the trade unionists who form the majority, it is very difficult to believe that, in the event of the return of a full majority of Labour members they would be permitted to sacrifice immediate trade union aims and ends to the fuller policy of economic democracy, involving a direct challenge to the power of the owning classes.

* * * * *

From this excursion into the wide and wild field, or jungle, of recent politics, I will return for a brief moment to trace the thread of my personal thinking and writing in its endeavour to adjust itself to these important happenings. It belongs to the half-conscious enfeeblement of age to dwell upon the more active and adventurous activities of youth, and to claim for them, when possible, some fruits of fulfilment. It is in this spirit that I am disposed to take my readers back into the statement of my early heresy of "oversaving" and to exaggerate whatever credit it may deserve as a contributory explanation of the grave issues of the present day. "Over-saving," in the sense of the attempt to create more capital than can profitably or even possibly be used for the supply of an increased rate of consumption, restricted by such over-saving, has been found to operate in two dangerous and damaging ways. One of these is the economic Imperialism by which the diplomatic and forcible power of the National Government is utilized by business pressures for the acquisition of colonies, protectorates, spheres of influence, in order to absorb profitably the excessive capital which "over-saving" seeks to create. The other is the cyclical depression which expresses the failure to find employment, either through expansion of home markets or by economic Imperialism, for the body of increased savings brought into existence in periods of full industrial activity. It is, of course, true that it is not necessary to own a country in order to invest capital in it, and a large proportion of our overseas investments in the nineteenth century went into South American and Asiatic countries which we did not politically control. But none the less it is advantageous to the investors of a capitalist country to plant their surplus capital in colonies or protectorates where their political control gives a measure of security and where public contracts and other lucrative business tend to "follow the flag." This aspect of investment has taken sharper shape in a world where economic nationalism has closed to foreigners many countries formerly open to their trade and capital, and where it is increasingly important to deal with countries which are bound to accept the modes of payment most convenient to the payee. Alike, then, for profitable investment and for essential import trade, colonies, protectorates, spheres of influence, have come to play an increasing part in the relations between the "have" and "have not" nations. It is simple folly to pretend that world-markets are free and that foreign investments can be made with as much safety and profit in foreign countries as in the Empire.

The shrinkage in the proportion of backward undeveloped countries to advanced capitalist countries within the last two generations has visibly inflamed the conflict of rival imperialisms and has given a realistic flavour to the political ambitions of Italy, Germany, and Japan. This shrinkage of undeveloped areas is, however, also responsible for the size and duration of the latest and worst trade depression, and, if unchecked, remains a future menace. For with it goes a fuller development of the technique of capitalism in all the advanced countries. Though completely reliable statistics of income distribution for all these countries are not available, such statistics as are available seem to bring out very clearly the result, which economic theory would predict, viz. that under highly evolved technique the proportion of money income going as interest, rent, and profits to the owning classes is enlarged, and that in consequence the amount of saving that seeks profitable investment is greater than before.* Since both home and external fields of investment are insufficient to take up this growing volume of investable savings, much of it lies

* The parade of working-class savings periodically presented in our Press only conceals the growing maldistribution by its failure to produce for comparison the rates of saving among the non-working classes, and attributing to the former the whole of the Post Office savings which are largely deposited by non-workers.

idle temporarily, together with the labour which it would employ if it were invested. This is the first stage in a depression which spreads farther when the fall in prices, first of capital goods, then of consumption goods, renders much of the earlier production unprofitable and brings about a decline in the real and the money income of the community as a whole. In such a situation it is idle to argue that recourse to free trade and stable money would put things right. For the growth of the trade barriers and of the monetary instability is a natural and inevitable concomitant of the inability of a larger and more productive capitalism to find sufficient markets for its potential products. Under such circumstances it is not possible to get nations to throw open their markets to free imports and to come to the monetary arrangements which such free intercourse requires. A modern capitalism which can proceed unchecked when confined to a few nations cannot operate when it has spread over a large number. It must inevitably be brought quickly to a restriction in its profitable marketing by reason of an increase in its supply without a corresponding increase of demand.

The belief, which still prevails among some orthodox economists, that a removal of all national barriers upon import and export trade and upon international loans and investment, with a proper distribution of gold in order to stabilize currencies and exchange, would give full scope to the increased productivity of modern capital and labour and make the whole world economically secure and prosperous, ignores the basic cause of economic waste, viz. the insufficiency of the effective demand, the real income which goes to the mass of working-class consumers in every country. The contention that full freedom of trade and investment would improve the condition of the workers everywhere by raising the productivity of their labour, is not adequate to meet this difficulty. For it is not a question of raising the amount of workers' pay but of raising *the proportion* that goes to those who will spend it on consumers' goods. No increased freedom of commerce, investments, and other economic internationalism will avail to secure full and continuous employment unless a more equal and equitable distribution is achieved between the owning and the working classes throughout the world.

I have here only mentioned a few of the wriggles of argument by which the supporters of current capitalism have striven to prevent what they regard as unjust, dangerous, and revolutionary attacks on the rights of property and freedom of business and financial enterprise. Most of my later writing has been directed to an insistence that cyclical depressions are phases of an under-production due to under-consumption, that under-consumption being itself a necessary result of a normal distribution of national income which gives too small a share to worker-consumers who would employ it almost wholly in present or early demand for commodities, too large a share to owners who would try to save too much of it. If, as is likely, I have committed myself to a tedious reiteration of this thesis, I can only plead that its acceptance and embodiment in a public policy of equitable distribution still appears to me the only way of escaping a revolutionary conflict of classes and of nations. How far that equity of distribution requires recourse to socialism, communism, and other modes of State planning must depend in large measure upon the current economic structure of each nation, and its capacity of skilled, honest, and humane regulation of the economic resources in the standardized industries which satisfy the ordinary economic needs of its members.

CHAPTER XVI

A SUMMARY OF HUMANIST ECONOMICS

THE communist principle "From each according to his ability, to each according to his needs," might be generally accepted as the right rule for an economic society, if it could be made to work.

In a pioneer farming family, thrown upon its own resources and independent of all markets, such a principle may be realized, provided the parents are kindly and reasonable beings. Each workable member of such a family will be set to do the sort and amount of work which he or she can do best, and with least painful or injurious effort, as compared with the work of other members; and the food, clothing, and other products of this community will be apportioned to the different members in accordance with their several needs for the maintenance and improvement of health and strength and according to their capacity of enjoyment. A young child, a sick person, an old or infirm member, may contribute nothing and yet receive a considerable share of the product: the work of the wife and mother, much of it not "economic" in the strict sense, will be held completely to fulfil the condition "according to ability," and to justify the satisfaction of her "needs."

Such a communist economy may even be workable

in a large primitive family extending towards a clan. It may be approached in a group of persons marooned on a desert island, or even on a larger scale in a besieged town, or other grave social emergency where everybody is required to do his "bit" and only limited supply of food is available. Even a nation in war time may approach such a communism.

Why does this equitable economic system become inapplicable to a larger society living under normal conditions? Chiefly because of the size and complexity of productive operations and of markets which bring into co-operation large numbers of persons who do not even know of one another's existence, and have no regard for one another's welfare. The equitable principle of "communism" does not seem applicable to any large aggregate of working people, even in a self-contained city, or nation, much less in a co-operative commonwealth of nations. Indeed, the very name "commonwealth" comes almost to possess a derisory significance, in a world where the normal operative principle is that everybody seeks to get as much for himself and to give as little as possible under the circumstances of his economic life.

It is true that the acceptance of this self-seeking competitive principle is still held by most economists and business men to put out of action the communist principle as a method of efficient productive distribution and consumption.

Though "the invisible hand" is no longer invoked, it is still widely maintained that a close concern for one's own personal economic gain, in profit, interest, salary, or wage, is conducive to the maximum progress in production of wealth and its distribution on an equitable basis, making due allowance for certain deficiencies of opportunity.

I have contested the accuracy of this economics upon two grounds, the one theoretic, the other practical. By analysis of market processes I claim to have shown that there is no tendency for the various buyers and sellers to make any equal or equitable gain from the price at which they buy or sell. While this is, of course, admitted of a market where monopoly prevails, it is denied of "competitive" markets. But an examination of most "competitive markets" shows, first that buyers or sellers as groups are unequal in their bargaining powers, sometimes the former, sometimes the latter, being in a position of advantage, owing to the over or under production of the product that is bought and sold, as represented in the current market price. Secondly, examination shows that the gains of the several buyers and sellers are unequal, some sellers getting out of the market price a greater gain than others, some buyers getting out of what they buy a satisfaction of more urgent needs than other buyers. Distribution according to needs is not even approximately achieved by the ordinary higgling in a so-called competitive market. Everywhere inequality of bargaining conditions, based on differences of needs, is represented in different amounts of gain.

An increasing number of persons has recently come to recognize that the competitive capitalist system is not working according to the individualist theory, and that disturbance and wastes are occurring upon a scale far exceeding the minor wastes and friction that were formerly admitted as qualifications of the excellence of the capitalist system.

The nature of a trade depression prevalent in nearly all industries, manufacturing, extractive, agricultural, commercial, financial, and in nearly all countries, is no longer held to be explained satisfactorily by such terms as post-war disturbance of trade and currency, economic nationalism with its tariffs and subsidies, though these occurrences undoubtedly contribute to worsen the situation. Both here and in America many open-minded economists have come to accept the view that the under-production, or periodic waste of the productive factors, implies an inability of markets for consumptive goods and capital goods to absorb the potential volume of increasing productivity rendered possible by technological improvements over a widening area of the world's surface. The stoppage of productive activity, which announces a depression, is first seen in the constructive industries employed in producing plant, raw material, and power.* For the

* I hope that the later statement of my over-saving heresy has made clear the right distinction between over-saving and over-

consciousness of a coming depression first shows itself among business men and financiers operating in these industries, who recognize that their unrestricted activity will soon bring a glut of capital goods and an unprofitable price-level. The business man decides to close down part of his plant in order to maintain a price that will continue to yield a profit, or at any rate to cover costs of production. This is as far as the ordinary business man need look. But economists are recognizing that they must probe deeper into the cause of stoppage, and they find it in the failure of the demand for consumptive goods to keep pace with the growth of productive capacity. Though there are divisions of opinion among the economists who take this view, as to the part played by money and the credit system, the stoppage of investment and its testimony to an

investment. A nation, like an individual, may save any proportion of his income he likes without causing excess of investment or depression of trade, provided it can find an adequate internal or external market for the increase of capital goods or consumption goods into which his savings go. So long as savings continue to be employed in paying workers to produce more capital goods, in plant and materials, either for home use or for export, there is no over-saving in the proper sense of the term. It is only when some of the current savings cannot find a profitable investment, owing to the failure of consumer markets (home or external) to keep pace with the increase of producing power, that depression and unemployment set in. Part of the recent savings lies idle in banks, waiting an opportunity for investment, and the decline of profit which under-production brings about causes a reduction in the rate of saving and in the proportion of the aggregate income which is saved.

attempt to "save" more than can find expression in the increase of real capital have now won a wide acceptance. Mr. J. M. Keynes, though not in full agreement with my analysis, has paid a handsome tribute to my early form of the over-saving heresy,* and in America the publications of the Brookings Institute have delved deep into the connections between distribution of national income and the rate of national consumption, finding therein the causation of cyclical depressions.

The growing recognition that the distribution of income under capitalism, whether monopolistic or competitive, is a factor of growing waste and disturbance to the productive and financial systems of the economic world, is everywhere bringing Governments into the adoption of policies which are socialistic or communistic in their character. The usual avoidance of these terms by politicians cannot conceal the fact. Whether under dictatorships or democracies, the interference with competitive capitalism by wage and price fixing, tariffs and subsidies, by increasing expenditure on "social services" and increasing taxation of high incomes and inheritances, contain an implicit recognition of the desirability of checking the free-play of profiteering and giving "security" of work and livelihood to the masses. The gigantic waste on armaments which is going on no doubt inhibits any effective rise of real income for the people in most

* *The General Theory of Employment*, pp. 364–71.

countries, but it also interferes with the "saving" surpluses of the rich and diverts them into governmental expenditure which, so long as it lasts, helps to increase the employment and the income of the workers. Though this clumsy rectification of the balance between spending and saving is impaired by indirect taxation falling on the working-class consumers, it must none the less be regarded as a testimony to the defective working of modern capitalism, in accordance with the criticism contained in the under-consumption theory. The economics as well as the ethics of capitalism have now been punctured, and the economic world is virtually committed to displacing the private and blind enterprise of profiteers by some conscious ordering of industry under public ownership or control.

This public planning will not, need not, I hold, go all the way along the road to socialism or communism. For both production and consumption as human arts present, not a compromise, but a natural and serviceable balance between socialism and individualism. Up to a point human beings are alike, almost identical in their tastes and capacities for work and enjoyment. A certain amount of regular routine activity is acceptable to most of us in all the operations of life. Physical exercise, even of a specialized kind, may be put to productive use, without encroaching upon liberty or evoking either painful effort or boredom. Division of labour, in other words, is not a mere sacrifice of individuality to society. It provides an element of skilled routine which is good for a man, and "takes less out of him" than a working day of many varied occupations. Such routine, however, must not be allowed to go as far as it does in most wage-earners' working days. A shorter day is essential to human liberty and the development of personality. But it is by no means desirable that anyone should be free to "do as he likes" with all his time. It may be difficult to fix the length of the routine day for different sorts of labour, manual and mental. But some standard contribution to the work of routine mechanical production is rightly required of every able-bodied person. For only thus can the maximum human liberty for leisure with its free-chosen activities be reached.

If we turn from the producer to the consumer side of life, the harmony between common and individual needs is even more manifest. The routine, highly mechanized labour, which has been so denounced by some apostles as destructive of human freedom, is justified by the fact that all men are alike and pretty equal in their requirements for the satisfaction of animal needs. The same sorts of food, clothing, housing, indeed the same sorts of comforts and enjoyments, express the real needs of most men and women, and these needs can only be adequately met by the routine labour I have justified upon its own account.

So far as this uniformity or standardization of man

is applicable both on his productive and consumptive side, it demands a scheme of social planning which shall produce the required goods and services at the lowest "routine" cost and shall distribute them so as to achieve the highest routine utility. Now it is idle to pretend that this planning can be left to a capitalism inspired and operated by private profit. The minimum cost and the maximum utility can only be attained by a conscious collective process, in the conduct of which the community as a whole must be the ultimate ruler. Most of the industries highly standardized in the processes of production and serving large bodies of consumers with standard goods, together with the equally standardized industries that furnish the plant, materials, power, and finance required by the first class of industries, must be "socialized" if they are to do their work economically and satisfactorily. The pursuit of private profit is not compatible with their service to the public. For in most of these trades the earlier uses of competitive profit-seeking, as a stimulus to economies and novelties and risk-taking, have disappeared, leaving large-scale businesses which are monopolistic or semi-monopolistic in their control of output and of prices.

There are, of course, a few industries supplying standard needs, that are not completely mechanizable. The group falling under agriculture is the most important. Some important agricultural processes do not admit complete social control, but are best left to the free profitable enterprise of peasant-farmers. This is chiefly due to the fact that no two pieces even of adjacent land are identical in their soil and situation. The same applies to animals upon the land. Irregularities of material and organic differences in vegetable and animal life demand the exercise of qualities in producers which may require incentives and rewards that are unnecessary where full routine is attainable.

What applies to agriculture is also applicable to other sorts of production where organic differences in shape and quality of important raw materials demand personal skill and judgment in handling them. Organic difference is, indeed, the term which best expresses the limits put upon routine production and routine consumption. For though, as we recognize, while persons may vary slightly in their demands for ordinary animal requirements, such variations may either be ignored or may be classified so as to find satisfaction by more specialized routine methods. But when we come to pronounced elements of individuality or personal taste, we reach the real limit to be set upon socialism. Individuality in consumption requires some corresponding individuality in production. A perfect fit in clothing calls for some personal skill in tailoring. In all the arts and crafts this natural harmony between skilled creative activity and individual enjoyment exists. But whether it be the qualitative differences of the material in a productive process or the qualitative differences of the consumer's needs, such processes are not amenable to routine mechanical production and call for private personal initiative, skill, and enterprise. They thus lie outside the proper sphere of collective industry that is passing out of private capitalism into State socialism, and remain a field for private personal enterprise with such profits, prizes, and other rewards as may be needed to call forth the necessary productive qualities of the craftsman, artist, or skilled risk-taker.

We find here the true line of cleavage between socialist and individualist activities. It is sometimes lightly assumed by socialistic theorists that a well-planned socialism can itself maintain the due liberty of research, personal freedom of creative expression and experimentalism, required for the skilled satisfaction of non-routine consumption, and that a sense of social service can operate as a sufficient motive for securing such skilled creative work. But the moral ideal of such service presumes a change in human nature as we know it that must take a long educational process to bring about, if indeed it is at all attainable having due regard to the deep-set character of the acquisitive and other self-assertive instincts. It therefore seems best to recognize that the routine industries form the right material for socialism, the skilled industries for private enterprise. If the prizes or profits of such private enterprise appear excessive, a careful process of taxation may be applied so as to curb such excess. I think that recent experience in business and politics is moving fairly rapidly towards a practical experimental acceptance of the division and the harmony here outlined. Where, as in the crude rapidity of the early Soviet revolution, the distinction was ignored, experience has already moved a considerable way towards redressing the initial error of a wholesale communism and restoring the serviceable incentives of personal gain and private control where these factors are found necessary.

But there are other issues which have occupied my long attention because they seem vital to a "humanist" theory and practice of economic life. The terms "cost" and "utility," which I provisionally adopted from ordinary business usage in order to present the conception of a balanced relation between production and consumption, demand closer investigation. For they have suffered a subtle vitiation, owing to that domination of the monetary measure which has been so hastily adopted by economic scientists as an instrument for converting economics into an "exact" science. For this purpose exact measurements are essential and the elimination of qualitative differences by conversion into quantitative differences. Now though our knowledge of the activities and the operations of the economic system has gained much by the application of statistics to the factors of supply and demand in market processes, the human appraisement of these processes cannot be achieved by such a method. "Cost," "utility," and "value" must find their ultimate expression in terms of desirable human life. Ruskin was perfectly right in his protest against the perversion of "value" from a vital into a merely monetary meaning. But "cost" and "utility" have suffered a similar perversion for the sake of getting economics into something like an exact science. The root error in such a process is the belief that, because costs and utilities are capable of comparison, the vital qualities which they express can be converted into quantitative measurements. The business man is right from his standpoint in measuring economic advance by reduced amount of costs and increase of amount of utilities, disregarding the human significance of both terms. But the economist, unless he accepts the post of intellectual servant of capitalism, has no right to adopt this scale of values and method of valuation. His rightful rôle is that of assessing "cost" and "utility," production and consumption, supply and demand, in terms of their contribution towards a desirable human life or a desirable society. Economic processes, thus regarded, constitute a fine art, and no science can reduce a fine art to a quantitative analysis. When J. S. Mill parted from the utilitarianism of Bentham and his own father by recognizing different qualities of utility, he went farther than he was aware towards a denial that economic or other social activities can become the subject-matter of exact science. Human life in all its related activities is an art and, while the physical and other organic sciences can supply knowledge to the practitioners of this art, they cannot make it into a science.

How, then, ought we to regard "costs" and "utilities" for the purpose of studying the branch of this art termed economics? If we repudiate the monetary measurement, how shall we estimate and compare costs and utilities? The human "cost" of anything regarded either from the standpoint of unpleasant or injurious human activity or "sacrifice," the human utility, regarded as pleasurable or serviceable consumption, will vary with different persons and with the same person in different times or circumstances. But how is it possible to compare the satisfactions and dissatisfactions of two or more different persons? To Professor Robbins this difficulty seems a sufficient ground for refusing to enter the world of personal feelings for economic estimates. Yet each of us is constantly engaged in performing the apparent miracle of comparing feelings and desires that differ in nature or quality and in giving so much time and energy to the satisfaction of one, so much to the satisfaction of another. This comparison which we perform involves, of course, some standard of reference. But this standard is a conception of some organic whole in a desirable life to which the different activities and satisfactions contribute in various degrees.

But though an individual person may thus effect a private assessment of his various costs and utilities, does it follow that a society can perform this operation? Even if we accord a "self" or other unity of thought and feeling to a social group, does that furnish any sound criterion for the apportionment of work and products on a human basis of desirability?

There is, moreover, a further issue which I have purposely kept in the background. Are we to take the existing estimate of the desirable and undesirable which each person holds, or some higher estimate of what is "good" for them, what they ought to and would desire if they had a more intelligent view of their real interests? In developing the principle of human costs and utilities as a basis for estimating the merits and defects of the existing economic system I have hesitated a good deal between these two estimates, seeking as far as possible to bring them into harmony by maintaining that the actual estimates which persons hold about the productive and consumptive operations are in substantial conformity with the estimates which they "ought" to hold and would hold if they knew their best interests. In two long treatises handling this subject, the former, entitled *Work and Wealth*,* relied upon the reduction of cost and utility into the actual estimate of individual producers and consumers, on the assumption that persons knew what was good and bad for them, and adduced natural support for this view. In my later treatise *Wealth and Life: A Human Valuation*, I laid more stress upon what may be termed "the higher accountancy," which would correct the personal

* George Allen & Unwin, Ltd.

errors of valuation that distorted tastes and misjudgments might make, by a deeper further-sighted and more social interpretation of cost and utility. This latter method receives support from the increasing part which the State and other public bodies take in the ordering of economic life and especially in the development of public services. For much of this public work and control is directed to secure for the producer and consumer, not what these persons actually desire, but what a public authority considers to be in their true interest, as members of a civilized progressive society. Many of the provisions for hygiene and safety in factories, mines, and workshops, and in the ordinary regulations for town life, do not express the current desires, knowledge, and demand of the mass of employers, employees, or citizens, but are imposed by more knowledgeable and expert authorities, often with the reluctant assent of those who benefit therefrom. The same is true of public education and of many modern provisions for dealing with defective mentality and other personal troubles which lie beyond the competence of the ordinary family. As a larger and larger share of the control of industry and expenditure of income passes into public hands, this imposition of a more informed and further-sighted public choice upon the less informed shorter-sighted individual choice alters our attitude towards cost and utility, the human character of which is endowed with less of the casual personal estimate and more of a longer-sighted social estimate. This is for many a hard saying, suggesting, as it does, not only the existence of a social mind, but of one that is higher and better than the individual minds that seem to form this social mind. How can the State know better than I what is for my good, and alter arrangements to my advantage? This is too large an issue for full discussion here. But it really turns upon the question whether the persons who act for the State in the matters under discussion may be disinterested experts. For all of us all the time are consulting and deferring to experts in matters which we know lie outside our personal competence. Such expertism is not confined to the skilled professions: it extends to a large area of our ordinary economic life as consumers. We take the word of persons in a position to know more than we can about many of the articles on which we spend our income. If, then, we approach the State not as a nest of bureaucrats or of interested politicians, but as a body of experts on matters where we can have little personal knowledge, we shall accept the view that the "costs" and "utilities" of economic life cannot be left for the estimate of their human worth entirely to the casual shifty tastes and desires of individual producer-consumers. But here a just protest may be entered. Are we then, it may be urged, to assume that ordinary human tastes and desires are not a true register of the inherently desirable? Are not the common estimates of what is good and bad in methods of work and of consumption sound, in that they register stores of human experience and satisfy the "natural" desires of man? Undoubtedly an affirmative reply must be given to such questions, so far as they relate to ordinary physiological rules. Though there is a good deal that is wrong and wasteful in ordinary diet and different people need different feeding, there are accepted standards for food and other physical requirements which must be taken as substantially sound. If expert physiologists and dieticians know of improvements, they had best proceed to introduce them by skilled education rather than by legal imposition. But because the use of alcohol may not be a matter for close regulation or prohibition, it by no means follows that dangerous drugs must be allowed a free market. While then it may well be admitted that some true relation exists between what a person wants and what is good for him, and that the use of "trial and error" is a legitimate mode of individual progress and adaptation to environment, there are important limits to this individual procedure. The case for public control does not, as some individuals contend, rest entirely on the necessity of preventing the freedom of one person encroaching upon the equal freedom of others. There is a need of public control in order to protect individuals on their own account from errors that are injurious or even fatal to themselves. This is a growing need in view of the rapid and important structural changes taking place in the material and social environment. The mentality of most individuals is quite incapable of a voluntary reasonable and rapid adjustment to those new conditions, and collective action is needed to safeguard them against the results of this incapacity. The simplest example of this need is the public regulation of road traffic. Here the individual is helpless to achieve security for himself and others, and a considered and compulsory social regulation is essential. Again, legal interference may be justified in safeguarding ignorant consumers against the propaganda methods of profiteering advertisers who push injurious foods and drugs upon them. Or, turning to the producer side of the economic process, it may be right to interfere with the working of overtime in certain industries where high rates of pay win the consent of workers who are prepared to jeopardize their health for increased income. Compulsory early-closing of shops is justified on similar grounds, for without such regulation one greedy shopkeeper by refusing to close may compel all his competitors to keep open when they want to close.

In all such matters we are dealing with the human aspect of "costs" and "utilities" and the need of protecting producers and consumers from the damages involved in a purely monetary valuation of these terms. There is, however, no general presumption that Society or the State knows better than we do what we want or ought to do. Social interference is only justified, as already urged, by the economy of standardization, in the sense that the desires and needs of people are similar in character and can best be met by social regulation of the productive and consumptive processes which satisfy these desires and needs.

So far as the desires and tastes of persons are so different as to defy this economy of standardization, their satisfaction should be and indeed must remain a sphere of private enterprise for the skilled personal attention and work of producers. This whole economy is based upon the assumption that as ordinary animals different persons are so much the same that their slight differences may be ignored, in order that those larger and qualitative differences constituting their higher personality may be supplied more abundantly with the goods and services they require. This is the familiar general truth that lower liberties may be suppressed in order to give ampler scope for higher liberties. The translation of costs and utilities from purely quantitative into qualitative terms is essential to this economy, and though it is impossible to measure the pleasures and pains, the subjective costs and utilities, of different persons, the assumption that "equality" prevails along the plane of standardized goods and services remains valid, and the productive processes involved in their supply rightly tend to become "socialized."

To a sound economy it is equally necessary that both "costs" and "utilities" shall be regarded from an organic standpoint. Anything that affects the workers' physique or mentality, such as increased or decreased strain of nerves or muscles by changes in conditions of labour, quicker or slower movements, longer or shorter hours, cannot be assessed in terms of human cost without reference to its effect on the human organism as a whole, taking into consideration all other economic or non-economic activities. The same principle applies to the utilities of consumption. The human utility of an article of consumption varies not only with the quantity of that article consumed, but with its effect upon other factors in the standard of consumption, individual or family, into which the particular article enters. The organic unity of man as producer and consumer renders invalid the statistical separatism which our neo-classical economics seeks to impose. This becomes apparent wherever the producer has the freedom and intelligence to envisage his life as a whole. As soon as the amount of work he does furnishes him with the means to satisfy his necessary or conventional standard of living, he will consider whether it is worth his while to do more work in order to add new comforts or luxuries to his standard, or to use his leisure time and energy in more agreeable and serviceable ways, some of which, such as gardening or arts and crafts, may have an economic value, others, such as reading and the pursuit of scientific knowledge, enrich his personality in non-economic ways.

These considerations make it evident that while a sort of economic science may be built upon a quantitative analysis which takes a separatist view of all acts of production and consumption, such a science cannot claim any ability or right to give authoritative direction to individuals or societies in the regulation of their conduct.

In the apportionment alike of work and income the most equitable rules could only assume that the abilities of production and the utilities of consumption of individuals and families were equal within the narrow limits of common physical and mental standards, mostly animal in the usual sense of that term. Beyond that level there can be no measure of equality in regulating work or income. So we return to the principle that the individual elements in personality defy alike a standard of production and of consumption and that any attempt to impose such a standard would be fatal to the highest kinds of work and of enjoyment, crippling progress alike in the economic activities and in the finer arts of human life. The enforcement of the common standard is the task of socialism which to-day confronts all democratic Governments. If the leaders of the socialist movement in all countries would recognize the limits of their rightful track, success, though by no means easy or rapid, would at least be relieved of some of its moral and intellectual obstacles. For though it might still meet the opposition of capitalism entrenched in powerful profiteering industries, it would no longer be exposed to the objection that it sought to repress all freedom of competitive enterprise in new and growing industries and to impose bureaucratic standards alike of work and enjoyment upon the various tastes of men, thus curtailing their freedom of choice at both ends of the economic process.

A public planning, such as we envisage, where a number of routine and key industries are owned and operated by expert officials while others, whose ownership and operation remain in private hands, are subject to working conditions publicly approved and to taxation of surplus profits, evidently demands a considerable departure from the conception of democratic government formed at a time when private enterprise prevailed throughout industry and public regulation was confined to a few humanitarian interferences. The amount of communism and socialism now admitted in most nations, together with the public regulation of wages, hours, and prices in private industries and the new conception and finance of social services demand a large place for authoritative expertism which conflicts with the loose liberty and equality that figured so prominently in the theory of democracy. I distinguish here the theory from the practice. For history makes it clear that the liberty and equality (to say nothing of fraternity) of eighteenth- and nineteenth-century democracy even in Britain and America were lacking in substance and that the real government remained in the hands of the upper owning classes. Nothing but the penetration of economic democracy into this class political democracy can make the latter a true instrument for popular liberty and welfare. But in order that economic democracy may function successfully it is essential that the general standard of intelligence and knowledge must rise to a level where a reasonable acceptance of special co-operation and expert direction is attained. The old notion that any ordinary man is equal to the doing of any job, or at any rate to judging how it should best be done, is still widely prevalent among the less educated classes. It must be displaced by a clear conviction that an effective operative democracy requires close attention to the inequalities in men in order that special abilities may be utilized for the common welfare.

APPENDIX

(cf. p. 142)

Both in England and America recent years have witnessed an important breakaway from orthodox *laissez faire* economics among some leading academic and other economists. Dr. Edwin Cannan came to discard the measurement of wealth by exchange-value and to insist upon equality of distribution of wealth and income (modified by differences of work) as the ideal of distribution.

Professor A. C. Pigou in his *Economics of Welfare,* though confining himself to that part of welfare which can be brought under "the measuring rod of money," takes a view of economic welfare (as distinguished from "total welfare") which leads him to insist upon the necessity of many forms of social interference in order to make the self-interest of individuals operate in socially beneficial channels. In his recent *Socialism versus Capitalists* he ranges himself with the Liberals of "Britain's Industrial Future" in assigning to public planning and State control a wide area of industry, using "the weapon of graduated death duties and graduated income tax, not merely as instruments of revenue but with the deliberate purpose of diminishing the glaring inequalities of fortune and opportunity which deface our present civilization—the industries affected with a public interest, or capable of wielding monopoly power, he would subject at least to public supervision and control." After the nationalization of the Bank of England, "If all went well, further steps towards nationalization of important industries would be taken by degrees" (p. 108).

Mr. J. M. Keynes, definitely assuming "The End of *Laissez Faire*," goes even further in his Liberal Socialism. His theory of interest enables him to foresee the way of getting rid of the scarcity of capital and the income paid for its use. He predicts the "enthusiasm of the *rentier,* the functionless investor," and assigns to the State the "socialization of investment" as "the only means of securing an approximation to full employment." Though "the central controls necessary to secure full employment involve a large extension of the traditional functions of government," they do not displace private enterprise or imply a general system of State planning.*

The significance of this breakaway from nineteenth-century *laissez faire* on the part of these economists may be distinguished from the attitude of several distinguished economists, with definitely socialistic attachments, such as Professors Tawney and Laski, with Mr. G. D. H. Cole.

* *The General Theory of Employment*, pp. 378–80.

INDEX